LEARN

HOW TO
DRIVE

AND
SURVIVE

LINDA ANN AZARELA
CERTIFIED DRIVING INSTRUCTOR

Learn How to Drive and Survive

iUniverse books may be ordered through booksellers or by contacting:

iUniverse
1663 Liberty Drive
Bloomington, IN 47403
www.iuniverse.com
844-349-9409

ISBN: 978-1-4502-3246-3 (sc)
ISBN: 978-1-4502-3247-0 (hc)
ISBN: 978-1-4502-3248-7 (e)

Print information available on the last page.

iUniverse rev. date: 11/16/2021

DEDICATION

This book is dedicated to my children, Heather and Blake, for always believing in me; my grandchildren, who will hopefully benefit from reading this book someday; to my mother, Rose Evans, who helped title the book and worked tirelessly photocopying and collating its hundreds of versions; to my brother Chuck Azarela for his computer support; to my cousin, Deborah Lofdahl, for her cover design suggestion; and to my Aunt Barb Azarela for all her encouragement and prayers. This book is also dedicated to my late sweetheart and best friend, Lenny Sances, for all of his love and moral support.

In addition, I wish to truly thank my good friends Jana Herdova for encouraging me to finish this book, Kari Henneken for faithfully helping me type and edit it night after night, weekend after weekend, for months on end (a lot of blood, sweat, and tears!), and my many thousands of teen and adult students whose input made the book possible.

My sincerest gratitude,
Linda ❤ ❤

TABLE OF CONTENTS

INTRODUCTION

"How can you *do* this job?" That's a question I'm asked every day. My various responses: "I'm obviously half insane," "*someone* has to do it," and "thank God for dual brakes!"

People also ask me if I believe in miracles. Well, I *must* -- because each day that I arrive home safely after doing eight hours of behind-the-wheel training is a miracle in itself!

Actually, it's not that bad if you really know what you're doing. And you have to truly be *on* the ball and have great reflexes. With my right foot resting over (but not on) the brake and a large rosary around my neck, I'm totally prepared!

A LITTLE BIT ABOUT ME

It continually amazes me that teaching Driver's Education is my chosen profession considering the fact that I was the *worst* driver as a teenager during the learning process. Remembering my horrible (what could have been deadly) Driver's Education behind-the-wheel sessions makes me wonder why I chose to teach Driver's Education for the rest of my life.

I remember doing the behind-the-wheel sessions on Tuesdays every week for three weeks after school. I remember being totally petrified and feeling really bad for my BTW instructor as well as my school chums who had no choice but to be in the vehicle with me.

The first Tuesday, I remember suggesting to everyone that they put on their seatbelts as snugly as possible because I had never operated a vehicle in my life (except a Barbie Jeep at a very young age). Some of the teens observing that day clung to the hand rest overhead as I readied myself to turn on the engine. I remember doing the sign of the Cross before I turned on the engine. Of course, I had no idea *how* to turn on an engine, so I asked the instructor, "Which way do I turn the key?" The teens in my car began cracking up with laughter, really making me very nervous. What kept going through my mind was, "Oh my God! I am responsible for all of the people in this car! Not to mention all the outside pedestrians and all other vehicles out there on the roads we will be traveling!"

After my instruction on how to start the engine (we were facing a fence), I proceeded to put the car into 'Drive.' *Big mistake,* since I really needed to be in 'Reverse' in order to go anywhere! As the teacher corrected me immediately, suggesting I move the gear shift (with my right foot on the brake) into R for 'Reverse,' I noticed his foot was on the dual brake as well, in fear that I may give it way too much gas and hit the car behind us. I did just fine, though, and proceeded to back out. (No skid marks either!)

As I pulled out of our high school parking lot heading east (about fifteen miles per hour in a thirty miles per hour zone!), I continued through the center of town, almost blowing right through a red light, just missing a pedestrian, and almost killing everyone in our vehicle since a huge Mack truck was also entering the intersection at that precise moment. My instructor almost had a coronary yelling at me. I thought he was going to stroke out! After a few short breaths, we proceeded with extra caution through the heart of town. Then, less than five minutes later, another 'minor' mistake – I almost went right past a stopped school bus (flashing lights and all) with about seven to eight kids being discharged from it. My teacher immediately brought the car to an abrupt halt -- I was sure I got whiplash at that moment! He then requested I remove my body from the driver's seat and get into the back seat. Another teen who had previously been observing me then began his lesson. There went the rest of *my* lesson – down the tubes!

Second Behind the Wheel Lesson (One Week Later): I got behind the wheel and went through the usual process of silent prayer. My instructor looked at me and said, "Oh, great! Just what I need right now! A basket-case driver." I felt truly offended – after all, we didn't die during our previous lesson and I hadn't killed anyone else, so why was he so cruel?

We (I) safely proceeded out of the high school parking lot without any disasters this time, thank God. For this lesson, he had me go west, towards the open country area, nowhere near the center of town. (I wonder why?) I drove for an entire twenty minutes and thought I did okay until one of the teens in the back of our car became car sick! I'm sure it had nothing to do with my abrupt braking prior to all of the harsh stops I had been making. After the ill teen gained his composure, we all proceeded back toward the high school. As I pulled in to do a final perpendicular park, I accidentally pressed the gas pedal instead of the brake and bumped the tall fence with the front of the bumper -- which caused the football team sitting on the ground on the other side of the fence to jump up. They began freaking out and yelling at me. What was their problem? They were on the other side! It's not like I hit them! (One of those football players went on to become a famous athlete – sorry, I can't mention any names!)

Needless to say, my behind-the-wheel portion of driver's education didn't go as well as I had expected. The remainder of my BTW was done in the classroom on a simulator, which to me wasn't any easier. Oh well . . .

A few months later, I finally completed the full thirty-six hours of Driver's Education and passed the course. I still didn't feel very comfortable as a new driver, so I practiced a lot with my boyfriend, who was far more patient than my Driver's Education teacher ever was. Thanks to him, I went on to become a very good, safe driver for the next forty years, totally ticket and collision free. Hard to imagine, considering how it all started, huh?

In 1983, I moved back home to the Midwest after being away for almost ten years. As I crossed the state line and began driving our famed and wonderful expressways again, I witnessed the crazy, zany, driving habits of hundreds of drivers here. It dawned on me at that moment what I needed to do – instruct driver's education and put safe drivers out on our roadways. The more, the better!

I became certified and worked for another driving school for a short while, then decided to open up my own driving school.

This truly has to have been my calling because I've now been instructing classroom and behind-the-wheel for twenty-seven years and am still going strong. For seventeen of those years, I owned and operated Tri-County Driving School, then sold it and semi-retired for the next seven years. I recently came out of semi-retirement and opened up Azarela Driving School in West Dundee and Elgin, Illinois. I have taught over 8,500 teenagers and hundreds of adults, all of whom are fine, to my knowledge, so I must be doing something right -- or I go to the right church because my prayers have been answered.

I truly wouldn't want to do anything else in this lifetime because this is what I love doing. Being a Driver's Education teacher is right up there with sky-diving and mountain climbing – very deadly professions, but someone has to do it and God chose me. Despite my rough beginning as a teen driver, everything turned out all right.

About ten years ago, I was at my old high school picking up two of my students when, while I was waiting at the front entrance, my old Driver's Education teacher walked by. I recognized his face, but the color of his hair, which used to be very black, was now all gray (not surprising, considering his profession and the interim time lapse). I said hello and he asked me, "Who are you?" I reintroduced myself to him, reminding him that he was my teacher over twenty years ago. When I said my name, he was shocked and said, "I can't believe you're still alive and well!"

He then reminded me of how I almost wiped out the entire football team. He asked what I was doing at the high school and I told him I was there to pick up my kids. He thought I was there to pick up my biological children. I told him the kids I was picking up were my Driver's Education students. He couldn't believe it! As my teen students approached me, my old teacher asked the boys, "Are you her students?" They replied, "Yes, and she's the best." He walked slowly away, scratching his head, but stopped, turned, and said, "What on God's green earth ever possessed you to become a Driver's Education teacher?" My response was, "Your great teaching, of course." I was being facetious. It was really because I wanted to prove to him that I knew I would be a super driver some day despite my unimpressive beginning.

I've been told by thousands of people that I am so good at my job and have so many stories to tell that I should write a book so I can help millions of folks of all ages. So here it is – so that you too can drive and survive.

RHYMES TAUGHT IN OUR CLASSROOMS

1. **If in doubt, don't go out.**

   Don't pull out from a side road until you are certain the road is clear in both directions. (That's good advice for dating situations, too! Teens, if you think you parents won't like the person you're thinking of dating, "don't go out" with him/her.)

2. **Take your time and you'll be fine.**

   In other, more famous words, "haste makes waste." If you are always in a hurry, you could cause a collision. Take your time and make thoughtful decisions. Remember, it's better to be late than to never arrive at all.

3. **Who's ever going straight, the turner must wait.**

   In general, anyone going straight has right of way over anyone making a left turn -- unless you are at a traffic light that stops oncoming traffic and you have a green left turn arrow. Another situation where this rule comes into play is at a T road. If you are the driver that has no road in front of you (on the stem of the T), any vehicle coming from the left or right has the right of way, not you.

4. **When in town, bring speed down.**

   This one is pretty obvious. Most towns lower speed limits to twenty-five to thirty miles per hour because there are frequent signal lights and pedestrians present.

5. **When in snow, go slow.**

   This may be obvious, but there actually is a law called

the "Basic Speed Law" that dictates that one must drive according to weather conditions, not according to the posted speed limit. If the speed limit posted is thirty miles per hour but the snow is coming down heavily, you may have to drive ten miles per hour. Tickets will be issued if you're caught driving faster than conditions warrant.

6. **Take heed; control your speed.**

   The numbers on the speed limit sign are there for a reason. That is the speed at which it is safest to drive in that particular place. On highways, you should drive at no more than fifty-five miles per hour (weather permitting) if you want to survive.

7. **Let them wait. It's okay to be late.**

   It's better to arrive alive than not at all. Don't drive hazardously to get to your destination; rather, plan better or leave earlier. It's not worth losing your life.

8. **Don't be a stinker. Use your blinker.**

   I am wondering if maybe they don't put blinkers in these newer cars? So many people don't use them! The law requires that you turn on your signals one hundred feet before you turn. (That's equivalent to three driveways in a residential area.)

9. **If no line, stop behind the sign.**

   On a road test, your front bumper must always be behind the white line when you come to a stop. If there is no white line, you must stop your front bumper before the stop sign. Before you proceed from that stop, check to your left and right to make sure it is safe to pull out. (If you cannot see because of an obstruction (a building or a bush blocks your view), you must stop a second time before proceeding through the intersection.

10. **If it's not clear, don't go near.**

    I refer specifically to flooded roads, a burning car, or some police situation. Obviously, it is smarter to avoid going near these, so, if necessary, turn your car around and take another route.

11. **If it's blurry, don't be in a hurry.**

    If inclement weather conditions cause your field of vision to be obscured, drive at a slower speed.

7

12. **If you see a fist, you must resist.**

    If a road-raging motorist tries to threaten you, do not get out of your vehicle. Do not make eye contact. Keep your windows closed and doors locked and get the heck out of there!

13. **When driving at night, stay closer to the right**.

    Whether on a four-lane or a two-lane road, driving to the right will lessen the chance of a head-on collision in case someone veers over the center yellow lines or causes *you* to veer because of their bright lights blinding you. You are much safer keeping your vehicle away from that center yellow line.

14. **Look to the rear when your car is in "R" gear.**

    "R" stands for 'Reverse,' and whenever you are driving in reverse, you *must always* look through the rear window to see where your car is going in order to avoid hitting another car or a pedestrian.

15. **Go slow and then go.**

    When turning left or right, in town or in the country, always go slowly into the turn, and then pick up speed after the turn, once your vehicle is straight.

16. **When gramps is close to the dotted white, you stay closer to the right**.

    On a four-lane road, some drivers veer over the dotted white line on their right because of their poor side vision. If you're in the lane to their right, you should stay closer to the white side line to compensate.

(NOTE: We've just created a 'rap' version of the above rhymes that we hope will be featured in an upcoming car insurance commercial.)

*THE 7-11 RULE**

I highly advise this rule to be followed at all times:

7 miles per hour on rainy, foggy, or snowy days;
11 miles per hour when turning corners on dry days.

*This is not about that place where you buy Slurpees and cigarettes, like many of my teen students thought!

REFERENCE POINTS

Perfect Right Turns -- Line up your body or right side mirror with the sidewalk and begin hand-over-hand turning for two and one-half full circles. Bring the wheel back another two and one-half circles when the car is straight -- and not before.

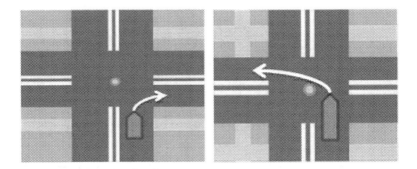

Perfect Left Turns – In urban areas, look for the manhole cover on most streets in the middle of the intersections. When the front bumper is even with that manhole cover, begin hand-over-hand turning for two and one-half circles. (If there is no manhole cover, begin hand-over-hand turning when your driver-side mirror is even with the double yellow lines on the road onto which you are turning. Bring the steering wheel back when the auto is straight – not before!

Perpendicular Parking – Line up your side mirror with the license plate of the car you plan to park next to, and then turn into the spot. The park is complete when your two mirrors are even with the car(s) next to you.

Exiting Angled or Perpendicular Parking – To prevent side-scraping another vehicle, always reverse halfway out of a parking spot before you turn your steering wheel in any direction.

Parallel Parking – Before backing into a parallel parking spot, make sure your passenger-side mirror is approximately six inches from the side-mirror of the front parked car.

Keeping Your Car Centered -- When driving, align your steering wheel over the dark oily strip down the middle of your lane.

Turn Signals – The rules specify that you turn on your right turn signal one hundred feet in advance of the turn. However, if there is a driveway on your right just before the turn (for example, for a gas station or strip mall), wait until you pass this driveway before turning on your signal to turn right. If you don't, a person leaving that driveway may turn out in front of you, assuming you are pulling into that driveway and not the signal light further ahead where you intended to turn.

Smooth Stops & Turns – You should start braking for a stop light or sign or turn you want to make about three driveways before that signal or sign or street in order to make a smooth and safe stop or turn.

TRAFFIC SIGNS & LIGHTS
AND THEIR SIGNIFICANCE

TRAFFIC SIGNS

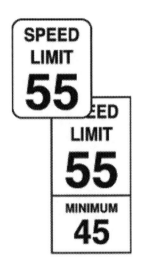

- Minimum speed limit signs on expressways will usually read forty-five miles per hour. Most expressways are fifty-five miles per hour. If you need to go less than forty-five miles per hour, you must have your hazard lights operating.

Right and Left
Turns Coming

Road Curves to
the Right and Left

Road Curves
to the Right

Right Turn
Ahead

Winding Road Ahead

Maximum Safe
Speed on
Curve or Turn

- Advisory signs give you directions when conditions change on the road ahead and you need to adjust your speed or be made aware. They show you how fast you may go around curves, for example.

- Red and white signs (also known as regulatory signs) tell you what you must do. Examples: "Stop," "Yield," "Do Not Enter," "Wrong Way," "No Right Turn," "No Parking," etc. (If you see a stop sign with an orange flag on top, it means it is in a location where there has never been a stop sign before.)

- Black words on a white background usually tell you what you CAN do. Examples: "Pass With Care" and "One Way." Speed limit signs are also black and white.

- Warning signs are yellow diamond shaped, with situation-particular drawings inside. Examples: "Pedestrian Crossing," "Cross Road," "Low Clearance," "Two-Way Traffic," "Merging Traffic," etc.

- "No Passing" signs are pennant-shaped amber-gold signs with black lettering.

- School zone signs are unique. They used to be an amber yellow color and are now fluorescent yellow so they are more visible. Now they cannot possibly be missed.

- Railroad crossing signs are round and yellow with a large "X" in the middle and black "R's." In country areas you might see the white and black crossbuck with the words, *"Railroad Crossing."*

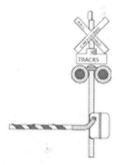

Interstate Route Sign   State Route Sign   US Highway Sign   Junction

- Route signs identify the road you are on. They are usually black and white in the country and red, white and blue on interstates. With interstates, a three-figured route that starts with an odd number leads you in and out of a city, and a three-figured route that starts with an even number goes around a city. An east-west road is *even*-numbered and a north-south road is *odd*-numbered.

- Construction zone signs are orange and black and either diamond or rectangle-shaped.

- Guide signs give directions to road services or points of interest and are usually in blue, green, or brown.

- International signs use pictures instead of words. They are similar to ours, but easier to understand.

TRAFFIC LIGHTS

- Red lights that remain on at intersections indicate that you must stop and wait. Red lights that are flashing mean that you must stop like you would at a stop sign and then proceed with caution. All states now allow motorists to make right turns at red lights provided they have yielded to pedestrians and other cars before making the turn. There are, however, some intersections that prohibit such turns and will have a sign stating, "No Turn on Red." In some cases, you might see this sign with a "When

Pedestrians Are Present" sign posted underneath, meaning you cannot make that right turn on red until all pedestrians have cleared the crosswalk.

- Yellow lights mean you are required to prepare to stop unless you have already passed the point of not being able to stop. Yellow lights generally stay yellow in rural areas for about four seconds before turning red. In the city, they are generally lit for two seconds before turning red. (Always check your rear-view mirror before you make any sudden stops.) A *flashing* yellow light means you should proceed with caution.

- There are two types of green lights: stale green lights and fresh green lights. A stale green has been green for awhile and a fresh green light just turned green. If you see a stale green light, be prepared to slow and stop. A fresh green light would be cause to proceed with caution -- because you must check for someone potentially running a red light from the other direction. A green light does not guarantee you safe passage through any intersection.

ARROWS

- A green arrow shows you the direction that traffic must go. A green arrow pointing left means that it is a left-protected turn. Vehicles coming toward you cannot proceed through the intersection because they still have a red light. You will see green arrows pointing downward at large toll booths indicating lane usage. There are also right-turn green arrows indicating you may only turn right after yielding to vehicles and pedestrians, and green arrows facing upward indicating that you proceed forward after yielding to vehicles and pedestrians.

- A yellow arrow warns that a red arrow is soon to appear.

- A red arrows means that you must stop because you cannot go in that direction until the arrow turns green.

- A police officer's signals must be obeyed over the traffic lights. For example, if a light is red, but the police officer waves you through the intersection, you must obey his command. If the situation that warrants police direction is at night, they usually use fluorescent wands to direct traffic in order to be easily seen.

ROADWAY MARKINGS

Roadway markings are there for a reason – usually to give warning and direction. Here are a few:

1. Double Solid Yellow Lines down the middle of the road . . . No passing.
2. Dotted Yellow Lines down the middle of the road . . . Cars traveling in both directions may pass.

3. Solid Yellow Line next to Dotted Yellow Lines on YOUR side . . . YOU (Car 1, above) may pass and the other side (Car 2 above) may not. If they have the dotted line and you have the solid line, you may not pass and they can.
4. Solid white lines are used for visibility, marking the sides of the road.
5. Dotted white lines indicate lane usage.
6. A wide white line indicates a crosswalk where pedestrians can cross the street at any intersections. In some areas, these can be a light fluorescent green line in school zones.
7. Solid white lines also indicate turn lanes and straight lanes and include arrows and writing.

8. You should see the word 'school' written in large white letters (sixty inches tall) on a road in front of a school.

9. Yellow and red curbs . . . No parking.

10. Handicapped parking is indicated by a box with diagonal stripes with a wheelchair emblem in yellow or blue.

11. Rumble strips are corrugated strips used along the sides of country roads to alert you that you're veering off the roadway. Or you might see them embedded in the road as an alert prior to toll booths or stop signs.

12. The white diagonal stripes in front of a fire station are there to allow room for emergency vehicles to come and go. To park there would be blocking their access and it is a ticketable offense.

13. The white diagonal stripes on both sides of a railroad crossing are there for your protection in case of a train derailment. They also create a buffer zone to keep a vehicle away from the tracks in case it is rear-ended. If you stop within this white-lined area, you risk a ticket or, worse, losing your life.

YIELDING SITUATIONS

1. All emergency vehicles – police, ambulance, fire trucks.
2. Other vehicles which have the right of way.
3. Pedestrians, whether in crosswalks or not.
4. Four-way stops and uncontrolled intersections.
5. Big trucks. (Yield or die. You won't win!)
6. Funeral processions (a person's last right). You are not allowed to interrupt a funeral procession, whether it is five cars or a hundred cars long.
7. School buses that are loading or discharging passengers.
8. Students that are anywhere near school zones and crosswalks.
9. Flaggers in construction zones whose signs order you to "Stop" or go "Slow."

SPEED LIMITS & LOCATIONS

Alleyways	15 mph
School Zones	20 mph When Children are Present
Highways	55 mph - Unless posted otherwise.
Most Country Roads	35 - 55 mph
Towns & Cities	25 or 30 miles per hour
Parking Lots	10 or 15 mph

** In bad weather, always go slower. **

PROPER LEFT TURNS

When wanting to turn left:

1. Activate your left turn signal at least one hundred feet prior to the turn.

2. To await your left turn, stop at a place where your body is even with the driver of the vehicle that is waiting to your left at the red light. Or stop at a place where your front bumper lines up with the manhole cover that will generally be found in the center of the intersection.

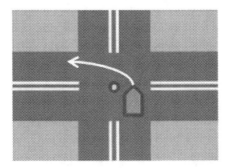

3. At the intersection, keep your vehicle straight while waiting to turn. Do not turn your wheels toward the turn because, in the off chance you are rear-ended, you could be shoved into the path of oncoming traffic (which could be deadly).

4. Once approaching traffic has cleared, or a yellow or red light stops oncoming traffic, slowly proceed with your turn. Remember to turn your steering wheel two and one-half times as you begin

your turn, proceed no faster than thirteen miles per hour, then bring back your steering wheel two and one-half times to straighten your vehicle. This puts your vehicle exactly where it needs to be.

PARKING

ANGLE PARKING - LEFT ANGLE

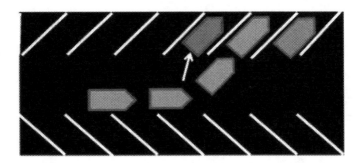

1. When angle parking on the left, aim your steering wheel just a hair to the right as you are approaching the parking spot you want.
2. When your driver-side mirror is even with the license plate of the car parked in the space just before the space you want, begin turning the steering wheel hand over hand two and one-half times to the left with your right foot pressing gently on the brake.
3. Pull your vehicle into the parking spot, keeping your foot lightly on the brake, and do not bring the steering wheel back until your vehicle is straight.
4. When it is straight, begin bringing the steering wheel back two and one-half times to the right, keeping your foot lightly on the brake.

5. Stop your vehicle at the top of the parking space (see #6 below), shift your car into 'Park,' and turn off the engine.

6. *Reference Point* - Because you cannot see the yellow line marking the front end of the space, stop when your body is even with the passenger front tire of the vehicle parked on your left and the driver-side rear tire of the vehicle parked on the right. (These reference points assume average-sized vehicles, so would vary if you were in a very short car and parking next to a much longer one.)

— EXITING LEFT ANGLED PARKING SPACE

1. Lock your car, put on your seatbelt, and start your engine.

2. Keeping your right foot on the brake, shift your car into 'Reverse."

3. Begin slowly backing up straight, always checking for pedestrians and other vehicles to which you must yield.

4. When your driver-side mirror is even with the rear bumper of the vehicle parked to your left (which assures that you don't side-scrape the car to your right), begin slowly turning your wheel two and one-half circles to your left, continually checking to your left, right, and rear. Once you've cleared the car on your right, keep your eyes looking out your rear window, and bring your car to a stop when it is completely straight.

5. Keeping your foot on the brake, shift your car into 'Drive.'

6. Giving the car just a drop of gas, turn your steering wheel two and one-half times to the right and proceed forward with caution.

ANGLE PARKING - RIGHT ANGLE

1. When angle parking on the *right*, aim your steering wheel just a hair to the *left* as you are approaching the parking spot you want.

2. When your front bumper is even with the license plate of the car parked in the space just before the space you want, begin turning the steering wheel hand over hand two and one-half times to the right.

3. As your vehicle is turning into the parking spot, do not bring the steering wheel back until your vehicle is straight.

4. When it is, cover the brake and begin bringing the steering wheel back two and one half times to the left.

5. Stop your vehicle at the top of the parking space when your body is even with the passenger rear side tire of the vehicle parked on your left.

6. Shift your car into 'Park' and turn off the engine.

— EXITING RIGHT ANGLED PARKING SPACE

1. Lock your car, put on your seatbelt start your engine.

2. Keeping your right foot on the brake, shift your car into 'Reverse."

3. Begin slowly backing up straight, always checking for pedestrians and other vehicles to which you must yield.

4. When your driver-side mirror is even with the rear bumper of the vehicle parked to your left (which assures that you don't side-scrape the car to your left), begin slowly turning your wheel two and one-half circles to your right, continually checking to your left, right, and rear. Once you've cleared the car on your left, keep your eyes looking out your rear window, and bring your car to a stop when it is completely straight.

5. Keeping your foot on the brake, shift your car into 'Drive.'

6. Giving the car just a touch of gas, turn your steering wheel two and one half times to the left and proceed forward with caution.

PERPENDICULAR PARKING (STRAIGHT PARKING):

1. When approaching a perpendicular parking space on the left, line up your driver-side mirror with the license plate of the car parked just before the space you wish to use.

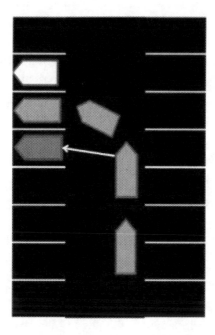

2. Signal a left turn and begin turning your steering wheel hand over hand over hand to the left two and one-half circles.

3. When your car is in the space and totally straight, bring back your steering wheel two and one-half times to the right, covering the brake to stop. (You'll know you're in your spot perfectly when your driver side mirror is lined up to the mirror of the car next to you. Knowing this reference point should prevent your car from bumping into the curb or cement block in front of your car and possibly damaging the front end of your car and fender.)

4. To complete this parking procedure, put your right foot on the brake and shift your car into "Park" and turn off your engine.

— EXITING PERPENDICULAR PARKING SPACE

1. Put on your seatbelt and start your engine.

2. With your foot on the brake, shift your car into 'Reverse.'

3. With your eyes looking through the rear window (to avoid traffic or pedestrians), slowly lift your foot off the brake and roll your car backwards until you are half-way out of the parking spot.

4. Still looking backwards, begin turning your steering wheel two and one-half circles in the opposite direction of the direction you will want to go.

5. Once you are out of your spot, put your foot on the brake and shift your car into 'Drive."

6. Before you lift your foot off the brake, bring back your steering wheel two and one-half circles as you proceed slowly forward.

REMEMBER -- You are not allowed to drive across the lanes of a parking lot. You must go up and down each lane properly to enter or exit the lot.

PARALLEL PARKING

Many people hate parallel parking because you must squeeze your vehicle in between two other vehicles parked along side a curb. It's really not as hard to accomplish as you might think. Here are a few tricks and easy steps to follow in order to park perfectly and be within three to four inches from the curb upon completion. (On most Secretary of State/Department of Motor Vehicle road tests, you should be within six inches of the curb, but closer is better.)

After learning this method and using my aforementioned reference points, most of my teens have learned to parallel park on their first try – and then went home to show their parents how to do it! Many parents were amazed at how fast their teens could perfect this maneuver. Many of my adult students who never thought they could parallel park were astonished when they too learned how easy it was and conquered their worst fears.

— STEPS TO A PERFECT PARALLEL PARK

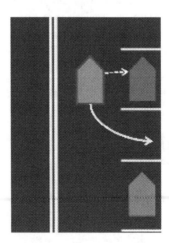

1. Pull your vehicle up next to the front vehicle, your right-side mirror about six inches from their left-side mirror.

2. Put your vehicle into 'Reverse.'

3. Slowly release your brake and use no gas.

4. Roll back slowly about four feet until your passenger mirror is even with the parked car's side back window.

5. Slowly turn your steering wheel towards the right, hand over hand, two and one-half times, rolling the entire time (no gas).

6. Then turn your steering wheel two and one-half times to the left, hand over hand, which should be placing your vehicle within six inches of the curb.

7. Once you are within four to six inches of the curb, straighten your tires to face forward.

8. Remember to cover your brake. If necessary, press lightly on your brake. Never use the gas because you might give too much and hit the front or back cars -- and that would NOT be good!

9. Place your vehicle in "Park" and turn off your engine.

10. If you are on a hill, set your emergency brake – but in the spring, summer, and fall only. Setting your emergency brake in the winter (if the temperature is or will be thirty-two degrees or below and the vehicle will be parked there for some time) could cause your brakes to freeze in that locked position, causing damage to your braking system. As long as your wheels are turned accordingly, your car should be safe resting against the curb.

11. If you are on a hill (facing up or down), turn wheels accordingly:
    a. "Up and Away" if facing uphill, or
    b. "Down and In" if facing downhill.

12. You have now completed your parallel park. *Please have your children exit the vehicle on the curb side because the street side is too dangerous.*

— EXITING PARALLEL PARKING

1. Before you start your engine, be sure car is in 'Park.'

2. If there is a vehicle still parked in front of your car, put your car into 'Reverse' (covering your brake) and roll back about six or seven inches while turning your steering two full circles toward the curb.

3. With your foot on the brake, put your car in 'Drive' and bring the steering wheel towards the street two full circles.

4. Signal to the left.

5. Since you are almost ready to pull out, check your blind spot by glancing over your left shoulder.

6. Go when it's safe to pull out.

7. Bring your steering wheel back a half circle as you pull away so you don't barge into oncoming traffic.

You've just finished a perfect park – Great job!

Another form of parking that is **illegal** is double parking. That is when you leave your car parked or idling (even briefly) in a lane of traffic next to someone already parallel parked at the curb. You can imagine how this practice disrupts the flow of traffic, especially in a busy city.

UP AND DOWNHILL PARKING

Up and down hill parking requires that your wheels be turned in or out when the park is complete. The reason for this is to prevent the vehicle from rolling down the hill and causing damage or death if bumped by another car or if the brakes fail. (Obviously, if this happened while you were parked on a flat surface, your vehicle mostly likely would not roll and cause such damage.) C.Y.O.B. means Cover Your Own Butt! Remember to always turn your wheels accordingly while up- or down-hill parking because if you don't turn your wheels and your vehicle gets bumped and pops out of gear and rolls down the street and kills someone, you stand to go to jail for involuntary manslaughter. Doing this is a requirement on a state test.

Every day I see hundreds of cars parked with their wheels not turned in the correct direction. I am constantly amazed at how seldom I see vehicle's wheels turned appropriately on hills. Nine out of ten drivers ignore this very important LAW and could suffer serious consequences due to their neglect.

To date, I've had over 8,500 students, ranging in age from fifteen to ninety-four, and have had them all practice about fifteen to twenty up- and down-hill parks during each of their many lessons. That's about 160,000 up- and down-hill parks I've taught so far, so now I can do these in my sleep!

— HOW TO DO A PERFECT UP-HILL PARK – WITH A CURB:

1. Signal to the right. (Remember, folks: "Don't be a stinker! Use your blinker!" Nothing bothers me more than motorists who are too lazy to use a turn signal. So many don't do it. I suppose it takes too much energy to use a ring finger to push a tiny little

lever downward or upward! Or maybe the auto industry forgot to install signals? Just joking!)

2. Start by slowly approaching the curb straight at about seven to eight miles per hour, with your foot off the gas and covering the brake.

3. Aim your steering wheel to the one o'clock position, holding it in this position for about three seconds.

4. When your front right wheel seems close to the curb, pull the wheel away from the curb, aiming your steering wheel to the eleven o'clock position and holding for three seconds.

5. Then bring your steering wheel to the twelve o'clock position. **(Suggestion:** *Use liquid correction fluid to put a small white arrow on the top of your steering wheel as a reference point. This helps with aiming your steering to the positions suggested above.)*

6. Once the arrow is straight up in the twelve o'clock position, put your car in 'Neutral,' turn your steering wheel two and one-half times towards the street, and let the car roll about five inches by releasing your brake. (No gas!)

7. When your tire touches the curb (this is okay on a state road test), put your vehicle in 'Park.' (Remember, never use your emergency brake overnight if the temperature drops to thirty-two degrees or below.)

— EXITING UPHILL CURB PARKING SPACE

1. Put on your seatbelt and start your engine.

2. Put your car in 'Drive' and keep your foot on the brake.

3. Signal to the left and check the traffic over your left shoulder.

4. When traffic is clear, slowly pull out.

5. Remember your wheels are already facing the street, so, as you step on the gas, turn your steering wheel two and one-half times to the right so you don't cross the center line into oncoming traffic.

You've just completed a successful uphill park with a curb.

— HOW TO DO A PERFECT UP-HILL PARK – WITHOUT A CURB:

1. Signal to the right.

2. Start by slowly approaching the straight at about seven to eight miles per hour, with your foot off the gas and covering the brake.

3. Aim your steering wheel to the one o'clock position, holding it in this position for about three seconds.

4. When your front right wheel seems close to the gravel or grass at the side of the road, pull the wheel away, aiming your steering wheel to the eleven o'clock position and holding for three seconds.

5. Then bring your steering wheel to the twelve o'clock position and press your brake pedal, bringing your car to a stop.

6. Put your car in 'Neutral,' turning your steering wheel two times to the right. (This pertains to up- and downhill parking when there is no curb.)

7. Put your vehicle in 'Park.' (Remember, never use your emergency brake overnight if the temperature drops to thirty-two degrees or below.)

— EXITING UPHILL NO-CURB PARKING SPACE

1. Put on your seatbelt and start your engine.
2. Put your car in 'Drive' and keep your foot on the brake.
3. Turn your steering wheel two full times to the left.
4. Signal to the left and check the traffic over your left shoulder.
5. When traffic is clear, pull out so you don't cross the center line into oncoming traffic.

You've just completed a successful uphill park without a curb.

— HOW TO DO A PERFECT <u>DOWN</u>-HILL PARK – <u>WITH</u> A CURB:

1. Signal to the right.
2. Start by slowly approaching the curb straight at about seven to eight miles per hour, with your foot off the gas and covering the brake.
3. Aim your steering wheel to the one o'clock position, holding it in this position for about three seconds.
4. When your front right wheel seems close to the curb, pull the wheel away from the curb, aiming your steering wheel to the eleven o'clock position and holding for three seconds.

5. Then bring your steering wheel to the twelve o'clock position.

6. Once the arrow is straight up in the twelve o'clock position, put your car in 'Neutral,' turn your steering wheel two½ times towards the curb, and let the car roll about five inches by releasing your brake. (No gas!)

7. When your tire touches the curb (this is okay on a state road test), put your vehicle in 'Park.' (Remember, never use your emergency brake overnight if the temperature is or will be below freezing.)

— EXITING DOWNHILL WITH CURB PARKING SPACE

1. Put on your seatbelt and start your engine.

2. With your foot firmly on the brake, shift your car into 'Drive.'

3. Turn your steering wheel two and one-half circles to the left (away from the curb).

4. Signal to the left and check the traffic over your left shoulder.

5. When traffic is clear, slowly pull out.

6. As you slowly step on the gas, aim your steering wheel to the eleven o'clock position and hold it for a few seconds, making sure not to cross the center line into oncoming traffic.

7. Once you have pulled out, straighten your steering wheel to the twelve o'clock position and continue driving.

You've just completed a successful uphill park with a curb.

— HOW TO DO A PERFECT DOWN-HILL PARK – WITHOUT A CURB:

1. Signal to the right.

2. Start by slowly approaching the curb straight at about seven to eight miles per hour, with your foot off the gas and covering the brake.

3. Aim your steering wheel to the one o'clock position, holding it in this position for about three seconds, coasting towards the gravel or grass on the right.

4. When your front right wheel seems close to that gravel or grass, pull the wheel away, aiming your steering wheel to the eleven o'clock position and holding for three seconds.

5. Then bring your steering wheel to the twelve o'clock position and press your brake pedal, bringing your car to a stop.

6. Turn your steering wheel so your tires face towards the grass or gravel on the right.
7. Put your vehicle in 'Park.' (Remember, never use your emergency brake overnight if the temperature drops to thirty-two degrees or below.)

— *EXITING DOWNHILL NO-CURB PARKING SPACE*

1. Put on your seat belt and start your engine.
2. Shift your car into 'Drive' and keep your foot on the brake.
3. Turn your steering wheel two full times to the left.
4. Signal to the left and check the traffic over your left shoulder.
5. When traffic is clear, pull out cautiously.
6. When you are half-way out of the spot, quickly turn your steering wheel one full circle to the right to avoid going into oncoming traffic and to straighten out the vehicle in the lane you want to travel.

You've just completed a successful downhill park without a curb.

TURNABOUTS

A turnabout is a maneuver used when you wish to change the direction in which you are driving. It is done using a cross street or a driveway. Keep in mind, turnabouts are allowed *only* in residential areas, *not* in the busy parts of town or at any traffic light intersections. The reason for this is that (1) turnabouts are very dangerous in these places and could be deadly and, because of that, (2) they are against the law and any driver making this mistake will be heavily ticketed for endangering not only his/her life but others' lives as well.

RIGHT TURNABOUT – This maneuver is usually done using quiet side roads or driveways because it so much simpler and safer than using an intersection, where you would have to back across two lanes of traffic. Because of the potential risk, this is not a very popular option, and I really wouldn't advise you doing it unless you absolutely have to.

— STEPS TO DO A PERFECT RIGHT TURNABOUT

1. Signal to the right.
2. Choose a driveway on the right.
3. Slowly pull into the CENTER of the driveway (approximately five miles per hour) so you're not near a mailbox or landscaping.
4. Stop the car when you are straight.
5. With your foot on the brake, put the car into 'Reverse.'
6. Before backing up, check to make sure there are no pedestrians or other vehicles approaching.
7. Start backing up, keeping your eyes looking through the back window the entire time.

8. Don't turn wheels to the left two and one-half circles until your driver's side back window is even with the middle of the road. (This places your vehicle on the proper side of the road.)

9. Once your car is straight in the proper lane, put your foot on the brake and bring your car to a stop.

10. Shift your car into 'Drive.'

11. As you give gas to proceed, bring your steering wheel back two and one-half circles and proceed cautiously.

You've just completed a Right Turnabout!

LEFT TURNABOUT - Remember, never do turnabouts at busy intersections (or anywhere there are signal lights). They are not permitted.

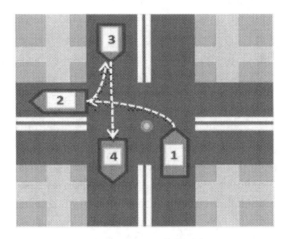

— STEPS TO DO A PERFECT LEFT TURNABOUT

1. Choose a street or driveway on the left.
2. Signal to the left about one hundred feet before turning.
3. Slowly turn left at eleven miles per hour into the street, keeping twelve inches from the right curb, or at five miles per hour into the center of a driveway, thus avoiding mailboxes or landscaping.
4. Stop the car when you are straight.
5. With your foot on the brake, put the car into 'Reverse.'
6. Before backing up, check to make sure there are no pedestrians or other vehicles approaching.
7. Begin backing up slowly (five miles per hour), looking back through your rear window the entire time.

8. Don't turn your steering wheel two and a half circles to the right until your body is even with the sidewalk. (This places your vehicle on the proper side of the road, approximately twelve to fifteen inches from the right curb.)

9. Once your car is straight in the proper lane, put your foot on the brake and bring your car to a stop.

10. Shift your car into 'Drive.'

11. As you give gas to proceed, bring your steering wheel back two and one-half circles to the left and proceed cautiously.

You have just successfully completed a Left Turnabout!

THREE-POINT TURN

A three-point turn would be used in all residential areas (no traffic-lighted corners) in a situation where you must turn your car around because of some problem with the traffic flow ahead. Examples: flooded road ahead, road block, road ends, etc.

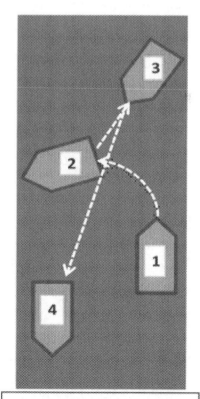

On Residential Roads Only!

— STEPS TO A PERFECT THREE-POINT TURN

1. Signal to the right, pull over to the right side of the road, coast over and prepare to stop. (Your foot should be off the gas.)
2. Signal to the left and check over your left shoulder for traffic.
3. When clear, press the gas pedal gently and quickly turn your steering wheel three full circles, aiming the nose of your car to the opposite side of the street, ending at a slight left angle to the curb.
4. With your right foot on the brake, shift your car into 'Reverse,' lift your foot off the brake (no gas) and roll backward slowly while turning your steering wheel three full circles to the right.
5. Bring your car to a stop when your driver side mirror is even with the middle of the street, then shift into 'Drive' and proceed with caution.

You have just completed a perfect Three-Point Turn. (Remember, never do one on a curve or a hill when in residential areas.)

REVERSE BACKUPS

With your right foot on the brake, put your car in 'Reverse.'

1. Place your right arm over the passenger seat.
2. Looking towards the rear window, begin by releasing the brake and giving it a touch of gas.
3. With your left hand on top of the steering wheel in the twelve o'clock position, keep the wheel straight and coast back as far as you are able to, no gas necessary. (On most state road tests, it's about one hundred feet backwards.)
4. Look behind you until you bring your car to a *complete* stop! (On a state test it is very important to look where you are backing the entire time you are in reverse.)
5. Then turn yourself around, put your car in DRIVE (with your foot on brake), and proceed when it's safe to do so.

PASSING SITUATIONS AND PROCEDURES

As you drive, there will occasionally be instances where you feel the need to pass another vehicle or obstacle in the road. This can be accomplished easily with practice. However, there are six potentially dangerous places where *no passing* is allowed:

1. On a hill;
2. On a curve;
3. Over railroad crossings;
4. Under a viaduct
5. Over a bridge;
6. At intersections.

Of course, there is no passing wherever there is a solid yellow line on your side or down both sides of the center of the road. Also, you must never pass a school bus with red flashing lights -- from no matter which direction (behind, oncoming, or either side).

Follow these steps to pass smoothly and safely:

1. Make sure you are in a passing zone (marked by a dotted yellow line down the center of the road). Unsafe passing zones are marked by solid yellow lines down the middle of the road and "No Passing" signs, which are pennant-shaped amber-gold signs with black lettering.
2. Make sure no one is passing you.

3. Make sure the way far ahead is clear of oncoming traffic and that there is no potential oncoming traffic from any side roads ahead.

4. When you've decided it is safe, signal left and smoothly ease your steering wheel to the left and change lanes. (Do not over-steer, especially as you accelerate. Doing so could cause your car to flip over.)

5. Accelerate enough to pass the vehicle ahead. You are not allowed to exceed the posted speed limit when passing vehicles.

6. When you can see the vehicle you have just passed in your rear view mirror, signal to the right, look over your right shoulder for a half-second glance to check the position of the car you're passing, then, if safe to do so, slowly move back into the same lane of the vehicle you've just passed. Do not check the position of the car you're passing by using your side mirror. Remember, objects seen in those side mirrors are closer in actuality than they appear. That's why shoulder checks are a must.

By the way, I recommend that you NEVER pass more than two vehicles at a time and never pass in bad weather. Each situation is dangerous and could be deadly.

BEING PASSED -- When someone wishes to pass you, your responsibility is to let them. Take these precautions:

1. Slow down, allowing the passer the extra space cushion they need to pass you. If you don't slow down, you could not only cause a collision in which you yourself would be involved, you could also be cited for causing it. Deliberating speeding up when someone is trying to pass you is highly illegal.

2. If the passer has used poor distance judgment and an oncoming vehicle appears to be too close for safe passing, you must stop your vehicle and pull off the road to allow the passer to return to the correct lane quickly enough to avoid a potentially deadly collision.

Please take a few minutes to adjust your side mirrors so that you have the most complete view of any vehicles approaching in the lanes next to you. To do this, while you are adjusting the mirrors in the driver's seat, lean as far left as you can to adjust the right mirror and as far right as you can to adjust the left mirror. This will eliminate the views of the side of your vehicle and expand the view of the lanes next to you.

SPECIAL TIPS

CARBON MONOXIDE

When approaching a vehicle stopped in front of you (with their engine running), stay far enough behind so you can see their *rear tires touching the ground*. That way, their exhaust fumes aren't being sucked up through your engine (which is like a vacuum). Exhaust fumes consist of carbon monoxide, which can cause headaches and death in some cases. It doesn't take much to poison a tiny infant in your car.

COMMUNICATING WITH OTHER DRIVERS

Use your horn to alert someone of a hazard, use your turn signals when turning and lane changing, use your parking lights and flashers when you have a disabled vehicle, tap your brake lights to tell a tailgater to back off, and back-up lights tell other vehicles that you are in reverse. It is not legal to flash your bright lights to alert oncoming traffic to the fact that there is police presence; however, you may flash your high beams briefly to alert an oncoming vehicle that his bright lights are on and blinding you.

GAS SAVING TIPS

1. When pumping gas, pump on the slower mode, not the quickest. When using the fast mode, air gets into the gas and you end up paying for air, not gas.
2. Try to park in a shaded spot as opposed to direct sunlight. Your gasoline evaporates in extremely hot situations.

PERSONAL SAFETY

1. When driving and when parked, always keep your car doors locked and any enticing valuables (purse, wallet, jewelry) out of sight (in the glove box, under the seat, behind the seat, etc.) to prevent potential car-jacking and/or robberies.

2. When driving in country areas, beware of deer crossings. When I was sixteen years old, coming home from work one night in my black VW beetle, a large grandpa deer – the biggest one I ever saw in my life! – jumped out and stopped right in front of my car. It happened so fast, I struck the deer. My whole car was smashed in, but the deer got up, looked at me and sneered (showing teeth), and walked away. I swear he was laughing at me because I got the worst end of that deal! So many young people die each year because an animal runs into their path and their gut reaction causes them to over-steer. *Never jerk your steering wheel at any speed over forty miles per hour.* That's how people die. The correct procedure is to (1) brake slowly, (2) slowly turn your steering wheel just a fraction of an inch, and (3) take your foot off the brake and hit the deer if you have to. (It's your life or the animal's life – which would *you* prefer?) Doing a screeching brake until you hit the deer will cause your vehicle's front to bear down and hit the animal low so it might be thrown up through your windshield after it is hit. Braking slowly then releasing the brake before impact will cause your vehicle's nose to raise and hit the deer head on so the deer won't be lifted and hit your windshield.

3. When you're in a nervous driving situation or are tired, try chewing some gum. It both relaxes your nerves *and* keeps you awake.

4. To avoid skidding or hydroplaning (skimming on top of any water on the road), lower your speed and keep your tires in good condition, with enough tread on them to provide traction.

5. When you do feel your tires skidding, always turn your steering wheel in the direction of the skid. Skidding on a curve is a most dangerous situation because you will most likely go off the road, which could be deadly. Try to correct the skid by keeping calm and slowly bringing your steering wheel back to your vehicle's intended path. Jerking the wheel back quickly could send you into oncoming traffic.

6. Be sure to wear your seat belt (whether it is legally required or not) because statistics prove that not doing so is extremely hazardous or deadly. Approximately 180,000 people incur brain injury every year and approximately 70,000 people a year receive spinal cord injuries.

7. If you experience a tire blow-out, keep a firm grip on your steering wheel and your foot *off* the gas as you navigate to the shoulder of the road. If the blow-out is to front tire, the car will pull in the direction of the blown-out tire. If it is to a rear tire, the rear of your car will generally weave from side to side. If, while you are trying to move to the roadside, you drift too far, don't jerk your steering wheel back to correct it because you could flip your car if you do. Slowly bring your car back straight onto to roadside.

8. Turn on your lights when the sun is even with the top of the tallest building or tree you see on the road ahead of you. When you turn them off is not as important as when you turn them on. Often folks drive without headlights when leaving a brightly lit area such as a gas station or a mall. Don't forget to turn them on at these times or a ticket could be issued or a collision could occur.

9. If you smoke, you are NEVER allowed to smoke anywhere near a gas pump for obvious reasons. You wouldn't believe how often I see this occurring. When I do, I approach the offender and ask them to please put out their cigarette in their car ashtray. If they get belligerent, I threaten to call the police. How arrogant it is to risk so many lives because you're too lazy to dispose of a cigarette butt prior to leaving your car?! Please do not put out your cigarette on the ground near the pump when you get out of your car. That's what your ashtrays are for.

10. If you are ever pulled over by someone you suspect is not a genuine police officer (perhaps flashing a fake-looking badge or driving an unmarked car with a single flashing red light on the dash):

    a. Lock your doors;
    b. Unroll your window just a few inches;
    c. Ask the officer why you are being pulled over;
    d. If he demands that you get out of your vehicle, don't do it. People have been raped and killed by getting out of their vehicle. (A genuine police officer would never demand that you get out of your vehicle in a deserted out-of-the-way area.

He would only request your license and registration and explain why you were pulled over. Remember our rhyme: "If in doubt, don't get out.")

e. Request that he summon another police officer onto the scene or ask him to follow you to a well-lighted area, preferably the nearest police station or the nearest store where there are other people nearby. (You have a legal right to make this request.)

f. If the officer still insists that you get out of your vehicle, call 911 on your cell phone and report the situation while driving yourself to the nearest police station. Try to get a good description of the person and their vehicle and its license plate number so that you can give this information to the 911 dispatcher.

MISCELLANEOUS:

1. Bright lights/high beams (the same thing) are needed while driving at night in rural areas because it is difficult to see well ahead of you. You must remember, however, to dim your beams when an oncoming car approaches so as not to blind the other driver.

2. Use your regular headlights (low beams) in urban areas and in the rain, snow and fog. Some vehicles are equipped with special yellow fog lights and others are not.

3. If you live near a toll way or are traveling cross country, remember to keep extra change in your vehicle at all times. Keep it within arm's reach so it is accessible when needed.

4. If you are carrying anything in your vehicle that protrudes a foot or more beyond your rear bumper, it must be tagged with an orange or red piece of material to alert driver behind you.

5. When I was a child, my six brothers and sisters and I would play hide and seek all the time under leaf piles at the end of our driveway in the street. As I got older and became a driver, I realized how dangerous, even deadly, this could have been for us. Never, ever drive through a leaf pile! You wouldn't want to go through the rest of your life knowing that you crippled or killed a child due to negligence.

ROAD RAGE

There are a lot of crazy, angry people driving on our roadways every day. I always advise my students:

1. To **always** control their anger and **never** make eye contact with another motorist who is looking to start trouble.

2. If you are ever in fear of your life or well-being, head to the nearest lighted store or, better yet, directly to a police station.

3. It's advisable to always carry a cell phone in case of emergencies; but remember that teenagers aged fifteen to nineteen are not allowed to use hand-held cell phones <u>while</u> <u>driving</u> (for calling or texting) unless it's an emergency – and then it had better *be* one. (The numbers 911 better be on your telephone's call register.)

4. Make sure your cell phone battery has been charged, so you don't run out of 'juice' (better known as battery power). Car chargers that you plug into your lighter adapter can come in very handy in case your phone does go dead.

5. Don't make it a habit to talk on your cell phone while driving unless you really need to because it can be very distracting. Being distracted could cause a collision and cause you to not notice a dangerous situation presenting itself until it's too late.

REMEMBER OUR RHYME: "If they make a fist, you must resist."

Here is a list of self-defense items you are allowed to carry in your car (in most states):

1. Mace – Use the small canisters about the size of a tube of lipstick. These can be purchased at most auto and hardware stores. Advisory: Mace is alright to keep in your car in cooler climates, but not in hot climates or in the summertime. The heat can cause the canisters to release fumes that can harm your eyes.
2. Scissors – You can use these to cut your seatbelt in case of an emergency, but they would be handy for self-defense as well.
3. The same can be said for a spring-loaded center punch (also purchased at most auto and hardware stores.) This tool is used to break side windows in case of an emergency, but can also be used as a self-defense mechanism.
4. A regular-sized flashlight. (The mega-size ones are considered weapons, so are not allowed in the cabin of the auto where people sit.)

Here is a list of some other things that are not allowed in the cabin of your car, but they can be carried in your trunk:

1. Baseball bat.
2. Chains.
3. Flares.
4. Nun-Chuks (a Karate weapon).

Here is a list of some things you cannot carry in the *cabin* of your vehicle under any circumstances (enforced by the law). They must be carried in the trunk (if at all):

1. Gasoline – This can only be carried in proper gasoline containers* and going a short distance to a stranded vehicle or to a residence to fill a lawnmower, for example. It is illegal to carry gasoline cross country for fear of running out of gas on a long haul. (*Empty gallon-sized water or milk containers are not the appropriate gasoline containers that some people think they are.)
2. Guns or ammunition weapons of any kind (unless you are a police officer). Other gun users, such as hunters, must keep their licensed firearms and ammunition in the trunk.
3. Blackjack (a heavy weapon covered in leather).
4. Dynamite or Nitroglycerin.
5. Bombs.

DRIVING UNDER THE INFLUENCE

If you want to end up in a morgue, speeding after drinking or using drugs is one of the fastest ways to get there.

In our state and in most states, the B.A.C. (Blood Alcohol Content) level for being considered drunk is .08 or higher. That would be equivalent to two drinks in the system of a normal-sized person within one hour. There is a slight difference between impairment and intoxication. Most people when pulled over and questioned by the police officer will admit to having had 'only two drinks.' If the officer feels that you have had more than two drinks, he can and will have you submit to a field sobriety test. Have you ever heard of the "Implied Consent" law? That means that once you sign your driver's license and drive, you agree to take a BAC test if asked to do so by a police officer. If you refuse, you are assumed guilty and automatically arrested.

If you are under twenty-one years of age, liquor in your system is illegal and zero-tolerance laws will be enforced – which means immediate arrest and license suspension. (The length of time your license is suspended depends on the severity of your intoxication level.)

It is a known fact that twenty-one year olds do the most drinking and driving each year.

Many people mix liquor or beer or wine with their everyday medications. This practice will adversely affect their driving ability.

Years ago, bars were able to advertise "Happy Hour" and "Two for the Price of One." Now there are laws preventing this practice because these signs enticed people to drink too much. Television and printed media also used to be full of alcohol advertising. Now, at least these advertisements do not show the actual consumption of alcohol.

The worst time to be out on the road driving is between the hours of 10:00 pm and 2:00 am on Fridays and Saturdays, and more so in warmer weather than in colder. Try to avoid driving during these hours unless it is absolutely necessary.

In our school, I have my students write an essay about why one shouldn't drink and drive. I also show numerous films on driving under the influence and the laws regulating impaired driving.

Approximately 28,000 people die each year on our country's roadways due to DUI, and millions are crippled or badly injured. My best friend's daughter-in-law was horrendously killed on Memorial Day of 2006 by a drunk driver with .24 BAC (three times the legal limit), leaving behind an eight-year-old boy now without a mommy. My best friend's son was positively devastated at losing his best friend of fourteen years (from early high school). This was the driver's third "Driving Under the Influence" (DUI) offense, and he didn't ever appear before a judge to answer for the second DUI, forfeiting the bond money paid to get him out at that time. Had he appeared for that second DUI and received some strong punishment for it, this death might not have happened and this boy would still have his mother. This collision and vehicular homicide netted the drunk driver only minor injuries and seven years in jail. Can you believe that? The DUI laws need to be made tougher because too many people keep getting away with driving under the influence.

One-third of all collisions are alcohol related, yet people who drive while intoxicated keep doing it day after day after day, ignoring the laws that do exist and the statistics. Don't make yourself one of these statistics. Please, please, please drive responsibly.

COLLISIONS & ACCIDENTS

Students ask me what the difference is between a collision and an accident.

- Most **collisions** were caused by driver error and could usually have been prevented. They are caused by inexperience, speeding, driving too fast for weather conditions, poor maintenance of the vehicle, and careless driving. Generally, someone is at fault.

- **Accidents** are totally unpredictable surprises; like lightening striking a tree and a limb falling on your car causing you an accident. Or perhaps an airplane falling from the sky and landing on your vehicle. These are true accidents, not collisions.

There are seven *major* things that cause collisions:

1. *Drunk-Driving* – This is the number one cause of collisions in our country. Anyone who consumes a large amount of alcohol in a short period of time loses their optimum motor skills, attention span, and judgment – skills that are all very necessary for safe driving.

2. *Sleepiness* – This is the second highest cause of collisions (next to driving while intoxicated). Lack of sleep can cause you to be, at the very least, not alert to potential driving dangers, which could cause a collision. At the most, it can cause you to fall asleep at the wheel, which could easily cause a fatal collision that could involve other people in addition to yourself.

3. *Speeding* – When you drive too fast for conditions, including your own "condition" (for example, driving under the influence).

4. *Right-Of-Way Errors* – When you either don't know or disregard who has the right of way.

5. *Left-of-Center Driving* – When you cross the center line heading into on-coming traffic.

6. *Tail-Gating* – When someone follows too closely behind you to be able to stop if you stop (or if you follow someone too closely). If someone is following too closely when you are approaching a traffic light or stop sign, quickly check your rear view mirror to see if that other vehicle will be able to stop without hitting you. If not, be prepared to continue on through that intersection, pull over to the shoulder, or make a quick right turn to avoid a possible collision. (Remember, the law says you may break a law to prevent a collision.)

7. *Distracted Driving Behaviors* – One in five drivers admit that they do distracting things while operating a vehicle. Smoking, spilled drinks, checking maps or GPS displays, changing CDs or radio stations, eating, attending to children, cell phoning or texting, shaving, reading, or applying makeup while driving are all typical examples of distracted driving behaviors -- which can very easily cause collisions.

— THINGS TO DO IF YOU ARE INVOLVED IN A COLLISION:

1. If possible, check all occupants in both vehicles to see if an ambulance is necessary.

2. Call 911 to report the collision (and ask for an ambulance if necessary).

3. Never move your vehicle if it is a severe collision. The police officers need to see the position of the vehicles involved. Only move them if the collision is a minor fender-bender and the vehicles are blocking traffic.

4. From the driver of the other vehicle, get their insurance information and the make and model of their vehicle.

5. Pay attention to the other driver. A description of their condition may be requested.

6. A description of the damage to all vehicles involved will be needed by the police and the insurance companies. Take heed.

7. Also note the weather and road conditions and the date and time of the collision.

8. To note all this information in one easy place, please see the "Collision Form" at the end of this book (and make a copy for your glove box).

The deadliest of all collisions is the head-on collision. If you are in a car going east at fifty miles per hour and you collide with a vehicle coming west at fifty miles per hour, the impact will be at one hundred miles per hour. As you can imagine, it would be unlikely that anyone would survive such an impact. This is a collision you must avoid at all costs, even it means driving into a ditch, which would more likely be an impact you could survive (especially if you are wearing your seatbelt as you should be).

Who is at fault in a rear-end collision depends on the situation:

1. If you are following someone and they stop suddenly and you rear-end them, you are at fault because you were obviously not keeping a proper following distance (four seconds).
2. If you are driving properly in your lane and another vehicle does an improper lane change, jumping right in front of you, cutting you off and causing you to rear-end him, that person is at fault.

Here are the odds of dying in a car crash as compared to dying in other ways:

- In a Fire: 1 in 45,000
- In an Airplane: 1 in 5,000,000
- By Drowning: 2 in 25,000
- By Car Crash: 1 in 135

Most of the people who are killed yearly in accidents and collisions are the younger drivers (between the ages of sixteen and twenty). They die due to lack of experience. Approximately 15,000 teens a year die in auto collisions. That averages to about eleven kids a day and is equivalent to about four large high schools with about 2,200 kids per school. Imagine walking into four different high schools on a Monday morning and not seeing one child walking the hallways – they all died over the weekend from partying and drinking. That's a pretty sobering thought (pardon the unfortunate wording).

Younger folks think it's fun to take down traffic signs (perhaps to hang them in their rooms), but doing so could cause a collision. Did you know that if you are caught taking down road signs, you could be put in jail for ten or more years, depending on the severity of any collision that may result?

I can honestly say that I've never had to attend the funeral of any of my 8,500 or so students because of auto-related collisions. Thank God for that! I must have done something right in educating these young people. The Lord truly carries our Driver's Education cars everywhere we go. Hundreds of times, we could have been killed by other drivers during behind-the-wheel lessons, but escaped injury. Thank the Lord for the dual brakes I have installed and have had to use -- a lot. (I lost count after a thousand!) I would have been dead twenty-seven years ago if it hadn't been for that extra brake on my side of the car!

FOR YOUR INFORMATION

Did you know that most collisions and deaths occur between ten pm and two am?

- Did you know that wearing seat belts reduces deaths up to 45%? Buckle up your seatbelt before someone else has to do it for you.

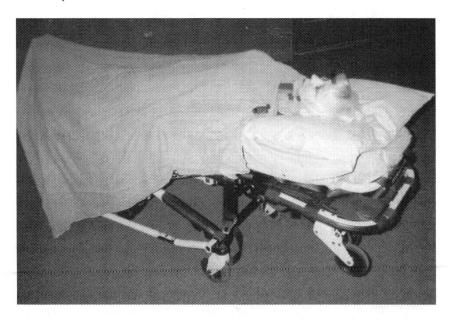

- Did you know that half of teenage deaths are alcohol related? And that the other half is due to reckless driving?

- Did you know that it is illegal to leave the scene of any collision in which you are involved and your license could be revoked for doing so?

- Teens, did you know that the laws are getting harsher and the insurance rates are getting higher because of your peers who brag and laugh about getting tickets? Don't laugh with them – knock 'em upside the head! They are preventing you from getting your license in a timely manner and costing you more money when you do get it.

- Did you know that, as a teen with just a driving permit, you are not allowed to drive between the hours of midnight and 6:00 am in most states (unless it is an emergency)?

- Did you know that if you are under seventeen years of age (in most states) and you drive after curfew hours, you must have a legal guardian with you in the vehicle? Breaking this law will get your license revoked.

- Did you know that two in five people will be involved in an alcohol-related collision?

- Did you know that approximately 75,000 police cars give chase each year?

- Did you know that approximately two hundred and fifty innocent bystanders are killed each year in our country?

- Did you know that if you see a personal vehicle with flashing blue lights, you should pull over and yield the right of way? The driver is most likely a fireperson rushing to the fire station.

- Did you know that when you're driving at dusk, you should stay closer to the right side of the road? If an oncoming vehicle veers over the centerline, you're much safer closer the right.

- Did you know that the road is much more slippery when it *first* rains (rather than later) because it mixes with the oils on the road which causes you to have less traction?

- Did you know that within the next year thousands and thousands more cameras will be added to city and suburban intersections in an effort to catch and ticket drivers who run red lights?

- Did you know that, while driving at night, your headlights allow you to see about four hundred and fifty feet ahead of you, but no more?

- Did you know that more teens are killed at night than during the day – even though millions of kids drive to school every day?

- Did you know that thirty-five percent of teen drivers admit to driving seventy miles per hour or higher on country roads and expressways.

- Did you know that black ice* will generally form on a winter road underneath an overhanging tree where the sun didn't shine?
    * Per <u>Dictionary.com</u>, "A thin sheet of ice, as on a road surface, usually caused by freezing mist and creating hazardous driving conditions."

- Did you know that ice forms on bridges faster because of the cold air circulating underneath the bridge?

- Did you know that it can be deadly to back up to a snow bank and keep your car running (as if waiting for someone) because the carbon monoxide has nowhere to escape but into your car?

- Did you know that at least five percent of all collisions involve animals, mostly deer, and generally around dawn and dusk, and more so during the months of September and October (hunting season).

- Did you know when a flash flood warning is issued or you are involved in one, you should look for higher ground, avoiding rivers, creeks, and ponds?

- Did you know that you should drive with your flashers on for visibility if a sandstorm erupts? After the sandstorm, don't forget to check and possible change your oil and air filters because they may be filled with sand and dirt, which will damage your engine.

- Did you know that you should never immediately remove the cap from your radiator if you suspect it is overheating? Wait until your car engine has cooled down (about fifteen minutes) or you may be scalded by hot radiator fluid?

- Did you know that if your car is more than a year old, you should begin to receive a yearly emission control notice in the mail with which you must comply? To do so, you merely visit one of many emissions testing stations and have your exhaust system checked. Though they may look like it, these notices are not advertisements for local sales like some people might think.

These are legal notices and you must comply or you may lose your driver's license.

- Did you know you should never use your emergency brake overnight in the winter if the temperature outside drops below thirty-two degrees? Your brake could freeze in that position. Even if you release it, it may still become damaged and burn out.

- Did you know that you must check your rear view and side view mirrors every six to seven seconds (just a half-second glance into these mirrors)?

- Did you know that if you are on a long driving trip and continually stare at the white lines down the middle of the road separating the lanes you can become a victim of "highway hypnosis," a trance-like state? To avoid this, keep your eyes moving around and try to focus more on the vehicles and road signs in front of you.

- Did you know that the law states you can break the law at any time if it means preventing a collision or hitting someone? For example, if you had to jump a curb and hit someone's mailbox or rosebushes to avoid a collision, it would be acceptable. No ticket . . . you would be congratulated. The insurance company would much rather pay for someone's mailbox than for someone's life or health.

- Did you know that teens are targets? They tend to drive newer cars, flashier cars, and sportier cars which are magnets for car thieves and other thrill-seeking drivers.

- Did you know that some elderly drivers suffer from poor peripheral (side) vision, so they often tend to use tunnel vision when driving? They do not notice safety markings on the road or potential hazards coming from the sides, tending to veer over white lane-dividing lines.

- Did you know you should never park within thirty-five feet of a fire hydrant? You must save enough space for a fire truck to reach the hydrant. A fireman has the legal right to break through your car windows if they need access to the hydrant you have blocked from their reach. Not only will you have window damage, but you will have water damage, a ticket, and possible fire hose damage, towing, and reclamation costs.

- Did you know that revving your motorcycle engine (disturbing the peace) will get you a ticket just as quickly as playing your music too loudly?

- Did you know that most gearshifts can't be moved unless your right foot is pressing on the brake pedal? This is a precaution so younger children can't accidentally move the vehicle by moving the gearshift.

- Did you know that, when backing out of any parking spot (angled or perpendicular), you should turn your steering wheel in the opposite direction of the way you want to go? But only begin turning the wheels after you are half-way out or you'll sideswipe the parked vehicle next to you.

- Did you know that when you see a flashing red traffic light, you are to stop for a moment and proceed with caution? Treat it as you would a stop sign. To know you've waited long enough, spell to yourself the word S-T-O-P while stopped.

- Did you know that gripping the wheel tightly could affect you later in life? Constant habitual gripping can cause arthritis-like pain. Some of my older students use what I call the "White Knuckle Death Grip" on the steering wheel – you need a crowbar to loosen their hands! (NOTE: You must hold your steering wheel FIRMLY, however, if you experience a blow-out in order to keep your car under control.)

- (This may seem obvious, but it bears mentioning.) Did you know that when you're following a vehicle and the driver brakes, **you** must brake, too, so you don't rear-end their vehicle? If you keep a following distance of three to four seconds behind a vehicle in front of you (in good weather), you should have enough space to get yourself out of any given situation. Allow more space (six to seven seconds) in inclement weather.

- Did you know that you are not allowed to go at a higher speed until your front bumper actually reaches the posted sign?

- Did you know that if you are driving in a residential area and you have yet to see a speed limit sign, you should drive no more than thirty miles per hour until you see a sign that says otherwise?

- Did you know that when two vehicles approach an uncontrolled intersection (with no traffic lights) from opposite directions at the same time and both want to turn down the same road or street, the vehicle closest to the curb or white line on the side of the road has right of way?

- Did you know that motorcyclists should ride to the left of the center of the road (which is usually an oily, potentially slippery line to avoid), not on the right side due to the frequency of potholes? If their tires hit a pothole, they could lose control and down the bike and be hurt or wipe out in your path and cause a collision.

- Did you know that it is illegal to drive without adequate liability insurance throughout our entire country?

- Did you know that it is not legal to cut through any private property to avoid an intersection with a signal light?

- Did you know that it is illegal to carry hot drinks in an uncovered container while driving? Lids are a must to prevent burns and then distraction-caused collisions.

- Did you know there are traction spots on various roadways? These are small grated and grooved areas that hold salt pellets in the winter and provide more traction to better grip the road.

- Did you know that the proper time to click off your turn signal on a lane change is just as your vehicle crosses over the white center line? Also, in most cases, you need to pick up your speed a little bit to make a lane change. It's not good to brake unless you have to.

- Did you know that floor mats (if not hooked under your seat) can roll up and perhaps press against your gas pedal, which could be very hazardous?

- Did you know that owning red and black flashy cars could cost you more for insurance coverage? Aside from being targets for thieves, the sportier ones are often used for drag-racing, and insurance companies have all the facts and figures -- therefore, they increase your insurance premiums.

- Did you know that a person can be ticketed going one mile per hour over the posted speed limit? You may get away with it in some areas, but in a school zone, the twenty miles per hour speed limit is strictly enforced when children are present. (If the weather conditions are bad – fog, rain, or snow, you will have to go even slower when children are present.)

- Did you know that the red and white striped bar that runs along the back of a semi-truck (from taillight to taillight) indicates that it is made of solid steel, and therefore can do a great deal of damage to our vehicles and our bodies if we were to hit it because our cars are not made of solid steel. Always keep a good four- to six-second following distance behind trucks.

- Did you know that it is illegal to block any business driveway in a city or town? You must allow an opening in case there is an emergency. For example, if someone has a heart attack when they see the price of gas at a gas station, the ambulance would need to get in to revive them (if possible).

- Did you know that you must be eighteen or over to legally pump gas without an adult present (at least in Illinois)? Check your local gas pump and you will see a sign posted there if it is the case in your state.

- Did you know that when you approach an uncontrolled T-intersection, the person on the stem of the T does not have the right of way?

- Did you know that you must always brake before a curve and again during the curve? There are signs posted as to the proper speed at which you are allowed to take that curve.

- Did you know that semi-trucks have four blind spots, two to the sides, one in front, and one in the rear? (Please see the diagram.)

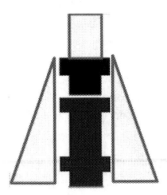

- Did you know that a semi-truck generally needs two lanes to make a left or right turn onto an urban street? Do not try to squeeze your vehicle past a semi. This could be deadly for you. You cannot compete and win with a vehicle this size.

- Did you know that most semi-trucks have air brakes which make it more difficult to stop going down hills? Consequently, there are runaway vehicle ramps that incline upward alongside downhill mountain roads to be used as escape paths.

- Did you know that children under eight years of age must use a child seat unless they are sixty pounds or over?

- Did you know that children under the age of twelve must sit only in the back seat? They are not allowed in the front seat because of potential airbag deployment, the force of which could kill them.

- Did you know that a person makes more decisions during two and one-half miles of city driving than a pilot makes flying an airplane?

- Did you know that driving in areas posted at twenty-five miles per hour (especially in the country) causes you to brake often, thereby wasting gasoline? (So why don't they get rid of the unnecessarily low-speed-limit areas if we are to conserve fuel?)

- Did you know that once a teen has a valid learner's permit, they are allowed to drive in other states as long as they are with one of their parents?

- Did you know it is illegal for you to pass on the shoulder of the road unless it is a major emergency?

- Did you know that in most states it is illegal to flip your middle finger at someone in public?

- Did you know that in most states it is illegal to use God's name in vain in public?

- Did you know that you could lose your license for three or more months if convicted of passing a school bus that is discharging or receiving children?

- Did you know that headlights are required when*ever* there is bad weather (rain, fog, snow, etc.)?

- Did you know that you never use your turn signals when backing up out of driveways or parking spaces? It is too confusing to oncoming traffic.

- Did you know that to avoid scraping your vehicle at a drive-thru (banks, fast-food restaurants, etc.), always make sure your driver-side mirror clears the post?

- Did you know that the proper procedure to use before crossing an uncontrolled intersection is to look left, then right, and then left again? Left is the side from which you would be more likely to get hit, so you should always check that side last before proceeding.

- Did you know that it's not good to let your gas level go below half a tank in the winter? Less could cause a fuel line freeze.

- Did you know that ABS stands for Anti-Lock Braking System? Almost all newer vehicles have ABS, which prevents your wheels from locking up in case you have to brake hard. Do not pump ABS brakes like you would the brakes on older vehicles.

- Did you know that if you have power brake failure, pumping your brakes could restore some of that braking power?

- Did you know that, according to Scott's Law, you should always move to the left lane if a police officer or police vehicle is on the right shoulder of the road for any reason? If you are unable to move over to the left lane, then you must reduce your speed to thirty five miles per hour or slower if necessary as you drive past his vehicle. If you don't, you can be cited and lose your license for up to ninety days or possibly longer.

- Did you know that in most states driving over thirty-five miles per hour in a construction zone can net you a $375 ticket at the first offense, a $1,100 ticket for the second offense, and a fine and jail after the third offense?

- Did you know that it's nice to be an organ donor so you can give another person after you're gone the life you no longer have? There are thousands of people on the donor registries, many of whom are infants and small children, who need donated organs to survive.

- Did you know that a new law in most states prohibits drivers of all ages from texting while driving?

- Did you know that it is illegal to use cell phones (calling or texting) or computers in your vehicle when driving in school zones or construction zones? (If you must, your car must be 'Park.')

- Did you know that when you are approximately 30 feet from an intersection when the light turns yellow, you must brake and stop (not hit the gas pedal, like most people)? Many intersections now have hidden cameras, and this is an offense for which you can be ticketed.

- Did you know you should never use your left foot on the brake and your right foot on the gas pedal at the same time in an automatic transmission vehicle? You might tend to ride the brakes, which can:

  1. Burn out your brake system,

  2. Confuse the driver behind you, and

  3. Assure that you'll fail your state road test.

  Your right foot should do all the work!

- Did you know that you must always park thirty-five feet away from any fire hydrant, allowing enough space for a fire truck to park? If you don't leave enough space, the firemen are allowed to do whatever they must to your car to reach the hydrant and put out that fire. In fact, it happened to a friend of mine. Her car windows were smashed in to run the hose through the car, the hose caused water damage to the gear shift and the whole interior of the car, she got a ticket for parking there in the first place, AND the car had to be towed because at this point it was inoperable. AND, because this was considered the fault of her own negligence, these damages were not covered on her insurance policy. Add to all that having to take time off from work for the court date and the additional money for court costs and she had to learn an expensive lesson. Unless you like throwing money away, don't let this happen to you. (I'd much rather go shopping with that money myself!)

- Did you know you should never ASS | U | ME? Because it makes an ASS out of U and ME. Don't ever *assume* that other drivers will do the right thing, because many drivers make mistakes, sometimes on purpose. Six out of ten drivers do the wrong things -- and here are some examples:

  1. People do not use turn signals when lane changing or turning. This happens all too frequently.

2. People forget to turn off their turn signals after turning so that, forty-four miles later, the person behind them is still wondering where the hell they are going to turn.

3. People do not turn into the proper lane when turning corners.

4. People do not yield right of way to other drivers – they cut you off.

5. People speed excessively and drive recklessly.

6. People follow too closely behind you – tailgating.

7. People incorrectly gauge the speed you are coming when deciding to pull out in front of you and then drive at a very, very slow speed.

8. People ignore stop signs, rolling right through them.

9. People pull into the space cushion you have allowed between yourself and the car in front of you.

10. People don't pull forward far enough past the white line on a green light to make a left turn, thus causing a traffic jam behind them.

11. People drive with two feet, thus causing their brake lights to be on all the while they are driving, annoying the drivers behind them.

12. At stop lights, people use the "turn-right-on-red" lane when they intend to go straight, thus preventing those who do wish to turn right from going ahead and right turning on red.

13. People do intend to turn right, but just sit there at the light until it is green, thus preventing others to turn right on red if they wish.

14. People attend to their cell phones (calling or texting), their meal eating, their newspapers or maps, or their grooming (putting on makeup or shaving) while driving, which caused them to drive too slowly or too erratically. I see this *all* the time! This is called impeding traffic, for which police officers are always on the lookout. Both driving too slowly

and driving too erratically are deserving of a ticket because they can cause deadly situations.

15. People seem to intentionally antagonize driver's education cars by pulling out in front of them when there is not enough time or space to do so just so they won't have to be behind them. These people must think we are miracle workers who can sprout wings and fly over them when they put us into these deadly situations. If *their* child were in our vehicle, they might think twice about placing them in such jeopardy. People, please be more cautious and courteous to all driver's education students. You had to learn at some point yourself, and I'm sure you didn't appreciate it when other motorists did that to you.

NOTE: If all the people in the world who make the above mistakes got their licenses revoked for making them, the roads would be *empty* and we would have less need for insurance because only the best drivers would be out there.

DRIVING THE EXPRESSWAYS & TOLLWAYS

Driving expressways can be very nerve-wracking because (1) you are driving at higher rates of speed than on most other streets and roads -- in fact you *must* drive at least forty-five miles per hour; (2) there are many more cars and trucks in such close proximity to you; which means (3) potential danger is always more imminent. However, in spite of all that, expressways and toll ways are safer than regular streets and roads for several reasons: (1) all traffic flows in one direction, with medians and barriers to prevent head-on collisions; (2) there is no cross-traffic because you must use entrance and exit ramps; and (3) there are no pedestrians, stop signs, or signal lights.

Unique to expressways, a "metered ramp" is necessary when many cars need to merge onto a busy expressway. It features a traffic light just before the expressway that shines either red or green. When there is an opening in the expressway traffic, the light will turn green and allow one or two vehicles onto the expressway at a time. If you proceed on a red light, you will be ticketed for disobeying the light because you could cause a collision because there is no opening in the traffic.

When about to enter an expressway, first check to see if there are any signs that say "Do Not Enter." If you see one, you are entering on an exit ramp, a situation that needs to be remedied *immediately* (!). This may seem obvious, but it is commonly known to us safe drivers that many people do not drive using common sense.

If you find you have taken an entrance ramp and you are going in the opposite direction than you intended to go, *never back up* on a ramp or an expressway. This is highly illegal. You must travel to the next ramp to exit and turn around.

When merging onto an expressway, the vehicle already on the expressway has the right of way. If you are that vehicle already on the expressway, do try to allow space for the merging vehicle to fit in by either speeding up or slowing down. By the way, when you are merging onto an expressway from a ramp, *do not* merge until your vehicle has passed the white point painted on the road.

A particular hazard with expressway driving occurs when on and off ramps are too close together and traffic must cross to get to their different destination. Remember while you are trying to enter the expressway that the vehicle already on the expressway has right of way, particularly since they are driving at a higher rate of speed. It is very important for all drivers to be courteous and to check their blind spots (*over their shoulders*) in this situation to prevent collisions.

If you experience any mechanical or medical difficulties while on the expressway, pull over to the right side shoulder, as far away from traffic as possible and call for help. (By the way, many expressways have call boxes every three to five miles in case you don't carry a cell phone.)

One thing I have noticed is that if you are driving along beside a semi-truck and look directly at the moving wheels and the axle you get a sense of vertigo that confuses your mind about the distance between yourself and the truck.

Also be aware that semi-trucks have four blind spots, two to the front and two to the rear. They are by the driver's and passenger side doors as well as near both sides of his rear axle.

There is one more situation of particular risk on an expressway – driving amid a cluster of other vehicles (known as a 'wolf pack'). Doing so leaves you no space cushion or a way out of a potentially dangerous situation. Although it is getting harder and harder to do these days with as many vehicles as are on our expressways, try very hard to keep your vehicle in an open area with a good amount of space around you.

Lastly, maximum speed limits on expressways and toll ways are generally fifty-five miles per hour, sometimes sixty-five miles per hour. However, many motorists travel seventy-five to eighty miles per hour on expressways. It is usually good to travel with the flow of traffic, but not at this high rate of speed. I know you don't want to be the one being ticketed for speeding because you kept up that high speed, so be the one who drives the speed limit and keeps everyone safe around them.

I have taught thousands of people to drive the expressways, but there is one person who comes to mind who still refuses to drive them even though she is completely capable of doing so. She'll take the long way into the city, braving hundreds of traffic lights to get there, rather than taking the expressway. She thinks it's much less hectic this way, when in truth it's about twice as hectic her way. (I taught Arden as an adult twenty-three years ago and she went on to become one of my dearest friends because she is a natural comedienne and I had such a great time teaching her.) Nevertheless, don't be like her, avoiding our expressways, because they are the safest fast way to get to your destination.

BEING PREPARED FOR EMERGENCIES

Items to Keep in Your Automobile Trunk at All Times:

1. First Aid Kit
2. Flashlight
3. Tool Kit
4. Extra Gallon of Windshield Washer Fluid
5. Quart of Motor Oil
6. Quart of Brake Fluid
7. Flares (two)
8. Small rug -- Useful for placing under your tires for traction in case your tires begin to spin in mushy snow.
9. Water -- For your radiator if it overheats and for drinking, in case you're stranded for a lengthy period of time.
10. Unsalted crackers or granola bars -- In case you're stranded and become hungry. (Salted crackers will make you thirsty, a problem if drinking water isn't available.)
11. Candles and Matches in a Can in a Plastic Bag – For warmth and light in case you're stranded. (One thing to remember, though: Don't burn the candles inside the car if your air supply is low.)
12. Extra Gloves, Hat, Boots, Raincoat and Blanket.
13. A Large Garbage Bag (or two or three) – To use as extra covering from the snow or rain if stranded.
14. A Long Red Ribbon -- To tie on your antenna in case your car is deep in snow or in a deep ditch.

15. An Old Shower Curtain or Plastic Sheet – To put on the ground if you (or anyone else) must lie down in the snow or mud to fix something under your car.

16. Window Scraper

17. An empty gas can. You may never travel with a full gas can unless it is secured in you trunk and you are traveling a very short distance.

18. A "Spring Loaded Center Punch" – A device you can purchase at any auto and hardware store, this is about the size of a pen with a sharp pointed end. If your car is ever under water, you can use this to break the *side* window of your car so you can get out (because electric locks won't operate when the car is submerged). Of course, this item should be kept handy -- in your glove box, not in the trunk.

    a. By the way, do not bother trying to use this device on a front window because front-window glass is much stronger than the glass used for side windows.

    b. The proper way to break that window is to hold the center punch like a ball-point pen in your left hand with your thumb at the end of it, and thrust it into the window at the center bottom as hard as you can while using your other hand to protect your face as you look away because the glass will shatter.

    c. Once your car is under water, do not try to open your door or windows because the pressure of the water rushing in could knock you unconscious. Wait until the car fills up with water and there is an air pocket at the top the car; then take a deep breath, punch the window, and swim to safety.

    d. If, for some reason, the window doesn't break, keep your head up to that air pocket and breathe until rescued.

    e. If you submerge, turn on your headlights – and not to be able to see the pretty little fish. It is so that rescue divers can see your vehicle's location.

19. Along the same lines, keep a cutting device (knife, scissors, etc.) handy in the cab of your car to cut your seatbelt in case you cannot make it release after an accident or submersion.

Though I highly recommend it for other folks, I can assure you that if *my* car ever went into deep water, the spring-loaded center punch would do me *no good!* You see, I cannot swim. I am, in fact, afraid of the water . . . so I'm sure I'd have a coronary and die instantly! I am not the swimmer my daughter Heather is (she learned life-saving at age ten) and my son Blake is (he was a Horizon League champion several years in a row during his college years and an Olympic Trials qualifier for the last two years.) But unless they happen to be with me when my car submerges, I am *history*!

Two good things can come out of having all of these things in your trunk (aside from their being useful in an emergency):

1. No one could ever abduct you and stuff you in your trunk! (There would be no room!)

2. All the junk in your trunk could be a buffer if you are ever rear-ended, potentially saving your life.

    (See? There's a method to my madness!)

HELPFUL SUGGESTIONS

1. Things to check before getting into your vehicle:
   a. Have your keys ready in your hand, with the longest key protruding through your fist to be ready in case of an attack.
   b. Look under your car as you approach it.
   c. Open up the driver's side door with your automatic key beeper.
   d. Look for suspicious people lurking around, either on foot or in any vehicles next to yours. (People in vans can abduct you because you are relatively out of sight.)
   e. Beware of anything near your driver's side door on the ground. It may have been planted there to distract you.
   f. Check inside your car for any unwanted passengers before entering it.
   g. If you do suspect anything or are afraid, go back into the building where you were and ask for Security or assistance with an escort back to your vehicle.
2. Know your vehicle and its capabilities.
   a. Know the size of your vehicle – how much space it takes to make turns (particularly u-turns) and to park.
   b. Know your entire instrument panel and the information it provides. Included are the vehicle's controls – ignition switch, turn signals, window washers/wipers, defrost system, cruise control, air conditioning, hazard flashers, high-low beams, and gauges.
   c. Steps to take when you get in your vehicle:

    i. Adjust the driver's seat to where you can comfortably reach the brake and gas pedals.

    ii. Adjust your rear-view mirror so you can see your entire back window.

    iii. Adjust your side mirrors so you can see anything approaching from both sides of your vehicle.

    iv. Make sure seat belts are fastened on all occupants, including you.

    v. Make sure the head restraint cushion is positioned firmly behind your head and neck.

    vi. Lock your doors. This will prevent car-jacking or theft of valuable items while you are idling.

    vii. Start your engine with the car in 'Park' and check your gauges – particularly the gas gauge and oil gauges. If either is low, it must be handled immediately. Obviously, your car needs gas to go; but your car needs oil like your body needs water. Without it, your engine will seize up and become a big piece of molten steel. You will need to replace your entire engine, which could cost thousands of dollars. (This actually happened to me when I was a teenager. No one told me to check my oil gauge and I paid the price for my ignorance!) Wherever you park your car overnight, check it in the morning for oily spots. If there is an unusual amount, investigate it.

d. Keep your front and back window areas clear of debris. In a collision, those things will go flying and could cause bodily harm.

e. Do not hang large items from your rear-view mirror – like baby shoes, stuffed dice, etc. It is illegal and you can be ticketed.

f. Keep your headlights and taillights clear and clean at all times. You usually don't need to worry about this, but you do in snowy and rainy weather or in muddy conditions.

g. Check at your local auto parts store for a beeping motion detector mechanism that, when installed, activates when something crosses your path as you back up (like a child or an animal or object in your way.) These come as standard equipment on the more expensive new cars today.

3. When driving past cars that are parallel parked, keep your car at least one door's width away. (Picture someone in that parked car opening their door to get out and your vehicle hitting them.)

4. *Always drive defensively* using the four C's:
   a. Caution
   b. Courtesy
   c. Common Sense
   d. Confidence
5. Never block an intersection waiting to make a turn or during heavy traffic (unless you have absolutely no alternative). It is against the law!
6. Never let another driver intimidate you into doing something either illegal or that you feel is the wrong thing to do at the time. For example, at a stop sign or light, don't feel you should pull out unsafely because the driver behind you is beeping his horn, obviously in a hurry. (Remember our rhyme, "If in doubt, don't pull out.")
7. When you are facing a school bus that is discharging a student at an intersection and you see a child fall in front of the bus (or stoop to pick up something dropped), don't sound your horn to alert the driver of a child he may not see. <u>Quickly</u> get out of your car and approach the bus with your hand up in a "Stop" position.
8. Try to keep to a minimum the amount of keys and gadgets you keep on your keychain. A very heavy keychain can adversely affect your ignition switch, eventually causing about $700 worth of damage. (I found this out the hard way and had to pay out of pocket to replace my ignition switch. This type of damage is not covered by your insurance plan.)

RAILROAD CROSSINGS

1. When approaching a railroad crossing with a moving train present, stop your car well behind the white line. If you stop close to the crossing arms or tracks and the train accidentally derails, you would be crushed to death. Better safe than sorry!

2. When crossing the tracks after the train has passed, double check to make sure no other trains are approaching from either direction.

3. Before you cross the tracks, use a tiny bit of gas to get started, but no gas or brakes while going directly over the tracks. Glide over the tracks smoothly. Too much gas can cause a blow-out in one of your tires, and too much braking could cause your brakes to lock. Either way, you could chance being stuck on the tracks!

4. As you clear the tracks, go back to the gas pedal and continue driving, or brake if it's necessary to stop due to traffic situations.

Never allow any part of your vehicle to be stopped on or near the tracks.

5. If your car does stall on the tracks, don't sit there trying to start the car. A vehicle can be replaced. Your life cannot. Remove everyone from your vehicle immediately and have them hide. If the car is hit by the train, there will be metal shards flying everywhere.

6. If your car stalls on the tracks and no train is coming, put your vehicle in 'Neutral' and push it off the tracks as quickly as possible. Hopefully, others will see the situation you are in and offer assistance.

7. *Never drive around crossing gates that are down!*

8. *Don't ever try to out-race a train!*

Did You Know That . . . ?

- A train going over a car is like a car driving over a soda can (flattening it)?

- Approximately four to five hundred people are killed at railroad crossings each year?

- A train a mile long can weigh approximately *ten thousand tons*?

- A train carrying hazardous chemicals derails somewhere in our United States every two weeks?

- A train can take up to one and a half miles to stop after applying the brake?

- There are over 250,000 railroad crossings in our country?

- Most people who are in vehicles hit by trains are usually within two miles of their homes?

- That railroad signs are posted approximately two hundred forty feet before the tracks in the city and approximately seven hundred forty feet before the tracks in the country? The reason they are posted closer in the city is because you are traveling at a slower speed. In the country, because you are traveling at a faster speed, the sign posted earlier gives you more time to slow down and see if a train is coming. Often gates are not present at a country railroad crossing so you must be more aware of an oncoming train than in the city.

- Radio/CD player/telephone headsets are never allowed to be worn while driving, especially near railroad crossings. (Ear buds are allowed.)

- When approaching railroad tracks, look, listen and prepare to stop if necessary. If there is not enough room on the other side of the tracks for your vehicle, do not cross the tracks.

- School buses carrying children and vehicles carrying flammable materials must always stop and check railroad tracks in both directions before crossing.

LATEST DRIVING LAWS REGARDING TEENS
(In Most States)

Though these are new Illinois laws, they will most likely apply in every other state as well.

1. A fourteen-year-old can now join a Driver's Education program provided they turn fifteen during the course.
2. A teen must have a permit in order to drive. This has always been true, but now they must hold it for nine months before they can get their license (as opposed to the previous law of six months).
3. A teen must now practice behind-the-wheel driving for fifty hours with a parent (as opposed to the previous twenty-five hours), but this could increase in the future. (And, parents, *please* don't yell at your teenagers when they are practicing. This will make them a lot more nervous and a collision could easily occur. I make it a practice never to yell at any of my students for this reason. When a potentially deadly mistake occurs, I have the student pull over, then calmly ask, "Now what did we learn from this experience?" (as I sit there feeling my heart about to jump out of my chest!)
4. Once they have a license, they must follow these rules:
    a. No driving from 12:00 midnight to 6:00 am all seven days a week, even with their parents in the car, unless it's an absolute emergency.
    b. No more than one friend (under age twenty) in their vehicle while they are driving for the first year, though siblings are permitted.

   c. Passengers ages fifteen to nineteen can be ticketed for riding with a new driver who is not legally permitted to have them in the car.

   d. Whether on a permit or a license, no cell phones are allowed in your hands while driving unless you are aged nineteen or older. Yes, this means *no texting* either! (In the city of Chicago – and perhaps many other cities – *no one*, regardless of age, can hold a cell phone in their hand while driving.)

5. Though not a new law, it is illegal to wear headphones while driving. Needless to say, having your ears covered in this manner impairs your ability to hear sirens, trains, tires screeching, etc.

6. Also not a new law, disturbing the peace with loud music, as teens are prone to do, is an offense that merits a ticket. In some cases, their vehicle can be impounded, which means taken away until they pay $250 to get it back. And it is a violation of basic human courtesy to require other people to listen to the music *you* like at the decibel level you like. Please be courteous to your fellow citizens. How would you like to pull up to a vehicle and have to listen to a blaring version of a 40's polka or a 50's bebop song? So why should the rest of us have to listen to your devil worshipping music? Unless you enjoy paying for peace disturbance tickets? It's just plain rude!

PREPARING FOR MOST STATE ROAD TESTS

Before you can take a road test, you must have either a legal permit or a valid driver's license, both of which require a written test to obtain. Recent statistics show that roughly 37.5 million Americans wouldn't be able to pass a written exam if they were asked to take one today. The statistics cite that the drivers who have the least driving knowledge to pass this test live in New York. New Jersey is second in line. Kansas drivers are the best at passing these tests. Could you pass a state written exam if ordered to take one? (My students certainly can. And they can pass it in 10 minutes' time, when it generally takes 30-45 minutes to complete the exam.)

The driver's license examiner will check the following items on your vehicle for working condition before beginning a road test:

1. Two headlights;
2. Front and rear signals;
3. Horn;
4. Two brake lights and two tail lights;
5. Bumpers;
6. Doors;
7. Brakes (service and emergency);
8. Gas pedal;
9. Seat belts;
10. Tires;
11. Muffler / exhaust system;
12. Windshields and windows;
13. Windshield wipers (if the weather is inclement);
14. Rear view and side view mirrors;

15. Front and rear license plates;
16. No loose objects in rear window;
17. Valid vehicle registration sticker on your license plate;
18. Proof of car insurance;

Following are most of the maneuvers you will be tested on during a twenty-minute road test to obtain a regular driver's license:

1. *Speed* – Try to stay under the posted speed by two miles per hour. If it's posted thirty miles per hour, go twenty-eight miles per hour (in good weather). If it's posted twenty-five miles per hour, go twenty-three miles per hour. This way, you don't chance speeding on the road test. If you go one mile per hour over what's posted, you could fail your road test. In bad weather, drive as slowly as necessary. Drive like a little old grandma or grandpa – slowly.

2. *Uphill & Downhill Parking* – Turn your wheels two and one-half times up, up and away on an uphill park. (Think of Superman -- he flies 'up, up and away'). On a downhill park, turn the wheels to the right two and one-half times down and in. Remember to signal left and check over your shoulder for traffic before pulling out. If you don't, it is an automatic fail.

3. *Left Turnabout* – Usually done on a side road in residential area.

4. *Reverse Back-Up* – Usually a person must back up about one hundred to one hundred fifty feet. Keep your eyes to the rear all the while you are backing up. Looking through your rear-view mirror is *not good enough*. It will be an automatic fail if you don't keep your eyes to the rear at *all times* until you have brought the vehicle to a complete stop.

5. *3-Point Turns* – These are always done in a residential areas.

6. *Stops* – Must be behind the white line at a stop sign or light. Must be a *complete* stop. (Count to four or spell the word S-T-O-P to yourself while you are stopped.) Then there is no question in the examiner's mind about whether or not you stopped long enough. But remember, if something is blocking your view, you will have to make a second stop, so be prepared to do so.

7. *Yielding* – If you do not yield to pedestrians and other vehicles, you could fail.

8. *Steering* – No open palms when turning the steering wheel or grabbing the wheel with an underhand grip. Unless you are

switching gears, do not take your hands off the steering wheel at all. You must drive with your hands in the ten and two o'clock positions or the nine and three o'clock positions (but no lower) with your elbows bent. Having your elbows bent is very important – it make it easier to do hand-over-hand turning to maneuver your vehicle in any situation and it is a *must* on any road test given by the state.

9. Most examiners would fail you if you use both feet driving an automatic transmission vehicle. Let your left foot go to sleepy land and just use your right foot for your gas pedal and your brake. I have many older drivers come to me for refresher courses, and I've noticed that they have a tendency to drive with both feet. They say they were taught that way back when. Unfortunately, that practice is no longer allowed on a state road test, so they must change their bad habits.

10. At the end of the test, you might be required to do an angle or perpendicular park when you return to the licensing facility. (We are lucky these days. Years ago, they required parallel parking. If that were still the case, most people wouldn't get their licenses – at least those people who haven't been taught by me! As you've seen, my techniques make learning this procedure so easy that my students succeed the first time they try.)

The things that are usually done wrong on a road test have different point values, like five, ten, fifteen, twenty, or twenty-five points. Each thing you do wrong is added up and deducted from one hundred. Which infraction causes how many points to be deducted is known only to the driver's examiners at the Secretary of State's office/Department of Motor Vehicle, but *you must pass the state road test with a seventy or better.* (This score might be different in some states.)

This may sound obvious, but when you take a road test, you always use your own (or a friend or relative's) vehicle. Vehicles are not supplied by the Secretary of State/Department of Motor Vehicle. There are two reasons for this: (1) You are more familiar with your own vehicle; and (2) if you use your own vehicle and do not pass, you cannot claim that the vehicle provided by the Secretary of State/Department of Motor Vehicle had something wrong with it or was unfamiliar to you.

Remember, it is generally a fifteen- to twenty-minute road test, but it will seem like the longest few minutes of your life!

Of the students I have taught, ninety-four out of one hundred who take the road test usually pass the first time. That's a fantastic percentage! Most of the six that didn't pass the test on the first try were able to go back the very next day and take the test again and then passed with flying colors.

If *you* didn't pass the first time, you should have come to *my* school! We cover everything under the sun. Plus, I offer refresher courses for all ages, but especially for the drivers older than age seventy-five who must be tested every year according to the laws of most, if not all, states.

There are very few driving schools other than mine I would recommend. In fact, some are downright questionable. One school that practices the high standards of teaching that are equivalent to mine and truly cares about their students the way I do is Clearview Driving School in Aurora, Illinois (and other locations). I know they are good because I personally trained many of their instructors!

ACTUAL LETTERS I'VE RECEIVED FROM PARENTS . . .

To the Manager of the School:

My daughter Stacy never felt comfortable sitting in a classroom, so we chose to home-school her for most of her school years. However, we did want her in a classroom for Driver's Education, so we called your school.

Stacy said she really enjoyed your classes and feels she learned a lot on how to stay safe while driving on our roadways. We highly recommend your school to others. Keep up the good work, and thanks for keeping our young children alive and safe.

Mrs. Thompson

Dear Miss Linda:

Thank you so very much for teaching our three sons in Driver's Education. After you taught our firstborn, we knew the rest must go to you, too. They can't say enough about you and how well you teach. I feel confident that they will grow to become very good drivers, thanks to you.

God Bless You,
Mrs. Smith

To the Best Teacher Ever . . .

That's what our daughters say whenever your name comes up. Thank you for teaching our children in ways we never imagined. Your rhymes have certainly helped them, and all of your reference points were something their father and I knew nothing about.

Keep up the great work!

Mr. & Mrs. Franklin

Dear Miss Linda:

I am very glad our son went to your school for Driver's Education instead of to his high school. We have known teens who have died learning from their public school, so we decided to have him take it privately.

Not only did you teach in ways we've never heard of, our son really caught on quickly and enjoys driving now, which he didn't ever want to do.

You also mentioned to the teens that God carries your vehicles in Driver's Education all the time. My son really didn't believe in God until he heard you speak of Him a lot. Now he even goes back to church with the family again.

Thank you so very much. You're the best.

God bless you always,

Ms. Janus

To the Owner of the Driving School:

Our two teenagers have gone on to become very responsible drivers thanks to your instruction. We as parents never worry about their capabilities since they attended your classes and behind-the-wheel lessons. They said that they learned a lot more with you than any of their friends did at their high school.

Thanks so much for caring enough about our kids to give them the best education. We sleep better at night since we chose this route. We will try to send our friends' kids to you so they too will be safe.

Sincerely,

Mr. & Mrs. Martins

Dear Linda and Staff:

I remember when I took Driver's End from you about 22 years ago. Now I have two teenage twin girls and am very glad you are still teaching because I want them to go with you, too. You did a great job with me, and I'm sure you'll do your absolute best with them as well. They are a little nervous, but I told them not to worry because you are a wonderful teacher and they will enjoy the classes.

I'll see you soon – at the first class. (I can't wait to see you again!)

Mrs. Pulaski

SOME LETTERS FROM MY TEEN STUDENTS

(Starting with my own two kids, who, by the way, got different and harder final tests than the rest because they had seen and helped me grade other kids' test papers through the years)

HEATHER – "The teacher is my mom. If you think she was easy on me, she wasn't. She made me do double – twice as much as the other teens had to do. Whenever I am grounded, I have to spend my time with her doing BTW observation. That's not fair. But, as she said, 'Life's not fair. Get used to it!'"

BLAKE (who didn't want the girls to know that his mom was the teacher, but they found out anyway!) – "I'm sure I'll be a good driver because I've been watching and listening to my mom (the Driver's Education teacher) since a very young age. Now that I'm fifteen, I think it will be easy. She's tough on me because I'm her child, so she made me do two courses and fifty hours of behind the wheel and observation when only twenty-five hours were mandatory by the state." ☹

BRITTANY D. – I loved this Driver's Education class. My teacher is cool and is very good at teaching us all we need to know in order to be good safe drivers. Thanks, Miss Linda. ♥

JERRY L. – My teacher, Miss Linda, and I have the same birthday, January 16th, so I got to take the course for free. Any teen born on this date gets it for free. Even if I had to pay for it, I wouldn't mind because it would be worth it. She's an excellent instructor.

SUZI M. – I couldn't wait for Driver's Education. I've been wanting to drive for a long time now. I was told about this class by a friend who loved it and said Miss Linda is the best teacher ever. So I asked my Mom & Dad if I could go here. And now they're happy I did, 'cuz, thanks to Miss Linda, I've taught them things they never even knew themselves.

JEFF B. – I never liked going to school, but this isn't like a real school. It's a lot better. My teacher helps us understand in easy ways by using special rhymes and things to help us remember. Thank you a lot, Miss Linda.

JENNIFER M. – Me and my sister (she's sixteen and I'm fifteen) are in this class together because we got a family discount and because your school came highly recommended by our school friends. They were right – you have cool ways of teaching so that we catch on quickly and learn a lot faster. Not only was the big book easy to understand, but the way you explain things made it even easier. Thanks a lot!

DEBORAH S. – This school is awesome! Our teacher, Miss Linda, teaches us with cool methods to make our driving and learning fun and easy. I am going to send all of my friends here because I want them to be safe, like I know I will be.

JOHN G. – I was not looking forward to going to classes at night after being in school most of the day. This is now my 5th night of class and I seem to be enjoying it. Now I can't wait to do the BTW (behind-the-wheel).

SARA F. – This class runs for fifteen nights, two hours per night and then we start the driving part of it. After learning what Miss Linda taught us, I am no longer afraid to drive. She makes it sound easy, so now I can't wait.

JAMES B. – Fun, fun, fun! And lots of cute girls in this class, too. I hope I can drive with some of them. I already know how to drive, so it should be easy. Miss Linda teaches us in ways everyone can understand, and she even taught things I didn't know. Wow, thanks!

MARSHA T. – This class is the best! My friends told me to come here, so I did. Now I'm glad I did because the way the teacher teaches us, it's fun and easy to learn. Now I'm not so afraid to drive. I'm actually looking forward to being in the car, as long as I can have Linda as my teacher.

SHERYL M. – Our Driver's Education. Class is very educational and interesting. I joined this class with my best friend and we just love it. We are also going to do the BTW together, too. There are a lot of cool teachers here (3 guys and 2 ladies). I want Miss Linda – no offense, Miss Janet. She's the coolest and smartest teacher I've ever had so far. Thanks, Miss L.

BRAD B, -- Lots of work, but worth it! Miss Linda is the greatest teacher I've ever had. She really knows how to teach. She should be the president of the country. She probably knows more than he does. She's real pretty, too.

CINDY T. – Miss Linda is a very fair teacher. She treats all of us kids the same. She also taught us self-defense in case we are attacked in road rage. She can really kick some butt! If she's as good in teaching in the car as she is in Karate, I'll be really happy learning from her.

DAVID J. – Our class has a lot of cute girls – and the teacher is not bad, either! Ha-ha. I am glad I joined this class because I need my driver's license and my brother went here and said I'd learn a lot. He was right – and I hate to admit that.

BETSY Q. – I joined this class with my best friend Sarah, and we love it. Most of the kids seem nice, and the teacher is great. She makes the classes fun, and you don't get bored like in regular school. The stories Miss Linda tells us are very interesting and informative. I'm glad I came here. Thanks, Miss Linda.

JOHN T. – These classes are very informative and interesting. Miss Linda knows what she is teaching, too. She uses a lot of cool ways to make us learn and understand. I should be a safe, good driver when I'm done with this course.

MARTHA S. – This class is a blast! It's not only fun, but easy to learn. I really like coming to my Driver's Education. Class four times a week. I know I will be a good, safe driver after these classes. The DUI films we saw make me really open my eyes to how bad it can be out on our highways. The laws should be a lot tougher on drunk drivers.

LYNN M. – This Driver's Education class is very educational. I've learned more here than I ever imagined. All the films we saw make it possible to see how bad it is to drink and drive. Miss Linda made us do a two-page report on drinking and driving statistics as part of the class. Many of my friends in this class learned a lot by listening to these reports. It certainly scared me into being a responsible driver. I don't want to be a statistic like thousands of others. Thanks, Miss Linda. You're super!

ALEX H. – I learned a lot from this class. The best thing about learning here was we were able to have conversations about everything (pertaining to driving). I liked how we went outside the box and actually did Karate demos (regarding road rage). I would definitely recommend a friend to this class and already have. The one and only bad thing was that no one from my school was here. Thank you, Miss Linda, for an awesome learning experience.

MIKE A. -- What I liked best about this class was that it was always up-beat. We didn't just sit there and have a teacher go blah blah-blah blah-blah. We learned what we needed to know and we had fun doing it. I also like driving the little new blue car. And the party at the end was pretty cool, too. The only thing I didn't like was doing the make-up work; but I really enjoyed the class otherwise.

LIZ S. – I learned a lot in Driver's Education. Class. Miss Linda is a great teacher and has taught me things that could really save my life on the road. She gives us little rhymes that are simple and easy to remember. I am really grateful that Linda was my teacher. I wouldn't want anyone else.

TRUE BEHIND-THE-WHEEL STORIES

Two male teen students I had in one class were best friends and took my course on the buddy system. (They observed only each other throughout all the BTW sessions, no other students.) On this particular occasion, we were driving on a high bridge over a river. I was assisting with the steering wheel to guide the car across the bridge (because I am deathly afraid of water, remember?).

My teen turned to me and said, "I can do it okay . . . I don't need your help."

I replied, "I help everyone over bridges, not just you, to prevent from going over the side."

My teen then replied, "It's okay. If we went in the water, I'd save you. I'm a good swimmer."

Just then, his best friend in the back seat said, "What about me? I can't swim either. Wouldn't you save me?"

The teen driver replied, "You can't get me a Blue Slip. She can!"

The best friend seemed offended, and I said, "Well, I guess friendship goes out the window when it comes to a driver's license!"

One day, three teens and I were driving the speed limit down Route 31 in Elgin, stopping at a red light, when another vehicle pulled up next to us at the light.

The lady inside shouted, "Learn how to drive!"

One of the teens observing in the back seat yelled back, "Can't you read the sign on top of our car? What do you think we're doing?" She had no comment and sped off as soon as the light turned green.

I then said to the teens, "The scary part is that she may *not* be able to read."

Then one of my teens asked, "How did she get a license if she can't read?

I replied, "Who knows how she got her license? Maybe she didn't even have one! Maybe she was driving illegally."

I was driving with three teens, two of which were boys. I noticed the driver was not checking his mirrors as often as he should and told him to keep his eyes moving at all times and get the big picture. His reply was, "I am keeping my eyes moving. Did you see those girls wearing bikinis in that yard we just passed?" I replied, "That's NOT what I mean by getting the big picture!" They all began laughing.

The oldest student I ever had was Fred P., who was 93 years old. He had lost his license because his neighbors complained he never looked behind him when he backed out of his long driveway. He called and asked if I could help him get his license back. I asked him why the state revoked his license and he said, "Not sure. The neighbors were complaining for no reason!" I decided to take the case, and, as we first backed out of his driveway, I had to remind him to stop before the sidewalk to check for pedestrians and traffic before backing into the street. He did just fine. As we drove down the street (very, very slowly -- ten miles per hour in a thirty mile per hour zone), he would have driven right through a stop sign, never even attempting to stop, if I hadn't used my dual control brake.

I said to him, "Fred, this is a stop sign. You must come to a complete stop."

He said, "Oh, that! I don't pay attention to these signs."

I said, "What! You have to pay attention to the signs on the road!"

His reply: "Well, they didn't have these signs here 80 years ago when I began to drive!"

I said, "Well, they do now and you must obey each and every one, especially the stop signs."

After two lessons with me, we felt that he was ready to try and get his license reinstated, so the next day we went to the Secretary of State's driver testing facility. He drove – about ten miles under the speed limit, in good weather! – all the way to the facility. As we approached the building, I reminded him how careful he must be to obey all the traffic signs on this road test.

He said, "I know, I know. I'll be okay."

It took us about ten minutes to walk from the car to the building about a hundred feet away. As we approached the front desk, the examiner, noting how slow he was walking, asked me why I brought him to their office. (They must have thought that because he walked slowly, he couldn't possible have the reflexes necessary to drive properly.) I told them the gentleman needed his revoked license reinstated, and the examiner looked at me with a look that said he thought I must have finally lost it (whatever "it" may be!).

I spoke up on behalf of my student. "Do you think I would bring to you in *my car* a client who couldn't drive? Just because he walks slowly, doesn't mean he can't drive!" The examiner finally said, "I hope you know what you're doing, Linda!" and two examiners proceeded to debate regarding who would be the one to take the man out for his test, tossing the clipboard back and forth between each other.

After about thirty minutes of waiting, his name was finally called to be tested. The examiner walked out to the car with Fred (another ten minute walk!) and I paced like a mother hen while he was out being tested. What should have been a fifteen minute test turned out to take twenty-five minutes. I was growing frantic. Finally, our car came around the corner – slowly, of course, but still in one piece. Fred completed his road test with a very nice perpendicular park, between the lines and everything.

The examiner stayed in the car for about five minutes, which is generally a sign of failure. So I thought to myself, "Poor Fred . . . " Then the examiner finally exited the car and came towards the building where I was frantically waiting. I asked the examiner, "How did he do!"

He replied, "Not bad! A bit slow, but he did okay." All this time, Fred was still walking slowly towards the building. Needless to say, Fred was able to get his license reinstated. He was very grateful for my help.

I heard only a few months later that Fred had passed away. Thank God, it was due to natural causes. He died in his sleep, not in a collision. I'm sure he's up in heaven now, probably irritating God by blowing off stop signs!

Though I always give it my best try, licenses are not for everyone. For instance, there were two female students during my entire teaching career that I was unable to teach, mostly due to their age. As much as I tried, it was not going to happen. So I politely suggested to them that it would be safer for all concerned if they stuck to public transportation. Fortunately, they themselves realized there was no hope and rightfully agreed.

SOME RHYMES FROM MY TEEN STUDENTS (and Me!)

When you drive, behave – or you'll end up in a grave!
If you don't want to die, don't get high.
Don't be a fool. When you drive, stay cool.
If you want to survive, don't drink and drive.
By Blake B.

If you're late getting out of bed, don't speed to get ahead.
If you want to stay alive, don't drive over fifty-five.
By Eric A.

If you are tired and fall asleep, you could get jumped by a creep!
If you drive with a buzz, you'll get busted by the fuzz.
By Sharyl G.

Don't drive with road rage. You could end up in a cage!
If you cause someone pain, you have nothing to gain.
By James C.

Don't make vulgarity a regularity.
I'd rather drive with the geeks and not with the freaks.
Take heed before your proceed.
To get to your place, don't make it a race.
By Tom H.

If you slow down at a yellow light, everything should be alright.
If you pay attention when you drive, you should stay alive.
By Elizabeth S.

Too much beer makes it harder to steer.
Any whiskey will make it risky.
Don't drive through a red or someone may end up dead.
If your speedometer is high, someone may die.
If you drive too fast, you may be part of the past.
By Alex H.

If you see a cop, be ready to stop.
Drive with only one friend or your driving could come to an end.
Christiana O.

When red and blue lights are flashin', pull over to the side in a timely
fashion.
Daniel F.

Always drive cautious so you don't make people nauseous!
Mark W.

Don't be mean – just go on green.
Mike M.

If you see a brother, sister, mom, or pop, you sure as heck better be ready to
stop!
If you don't stop at a railroad track, you might not live and never come
back.
Jessie Ahrens, Age 8 (Linda's Granddaughter)

Take your time, and you'll be fine.
If no line, stop behind the sign.
When someone is going straight, the turner must wait.
If in doubt, don't pull out.
When in town, bring speed down.
When in snow, you must go slow.
Take heed, control your speed.
Let them wait; it's okay to be late.
Don't be a stinker, use your blinker.
If it's not clear, don't go near.

If's it's blurry, don't be in a hurry.
If you see a fist, you must resist.
When driving at night, stay closer to the right.
Look to the rear when your car is in 'R' gear.
Go slow and then go.
Keep your license in your pocket or you'll wind up on the docket!
If you're in a school zone, you shouldn't be on cell phone!
If you're in a construction zone, you shouldn't be on a cell phone!
If you text, you could be hexed . . . or next!
When in rain, use your brain!
By Linda Azarela (the Teacher)

"Most of the above rhymes by Miss Azarela have been set to rap music and are available in CD form for $4.99 by writing the author at LAzarela@ comcast.net."

IN CLOSING . . .

Parents are always praising me and blessing me and admiring me for doing this job on a daily basis, sometimes four and five teens per day, at one and one-half hours each. Sometimes, I think it's more insanity than anything else. Being a Driver's Education teacher is as dangerous as mountain climbing or sky-diving.

About six years ago, I asked my insurance agent about increasing my life insurance coverage just in case I am killed while teaching. He laughed out loud and said, "Insurance companies don't like increasing policies on Driver's Education teachers because they hold deadly jobs." So much for increasing on my life insurance! My children (now adults) will have to make it on the little insurance I presently have. This is the only profession I truly know and enjoy doing, believe it or not. The teenagers keep me on my toes, and young at heart. Not young in my body, though, since I've aged a lot doing this wonderful job. But this is my calling!

Though I was the worst teen driver back in the early seventies, amazingly enough, I've never received a single moving violation ticket in my forty years of driving, nor have I caused any collisions (thank God). But, as I was learning to drive in high school, I was petrified and very unsure of my ability to ever be a driver -- let alone a certified Driver's Education instructor!

I actually received a Teacher of the Year award in 1997 from the over 1,000 teenagers attending several area schools. What an honor to know that what I've done has left an impression on so many young lives, that they thought enough of my teaching to award me this honor. I was very touched by their generosity and faith in me.

I've always treated my students as my very own, the way I treated my two children, Heather and Blake. I want all my children to live long, healthy lives so I taught them to the best of my abilities, and with the grace of God, hopefully they will all stay safe and enjoy their lives to the fullest.

Please remember all of your teachers. We're not heroes; we're just teachers -- but where would you be without us?

God bless you all and stay safe,

Linda

One Final Thought:
Remember: "It's not who's right; it's who's left."
(Think about it!)

GLOSSARY

A

Acceleration Lane – The lane used to merge into expressway traffic.

Active Restraint Device – A seatbelt or child seat that you yourself must put on.

Angle Parking – Parking your car on a slant.

Anti-Lock Braking System (ABS) – A devise installed on many new cars that keeps your wheel from locking if you slam on the brakes.

B

Back-Up Lights – Lights on the rear of your car that activate when you are backing up.

Basic Speed Law – You cannot drive faster than existing conditions permit.

Blind Spot – An area on the road that you cannot see in your mirrors.

Blood Alcohol Content (BAC) – The amount of alcohol in your bloodstream.

Blow-Out – When one of your tires loses major air pressure.

Braking Distance – The distance between when you apply your brakes and when you come to a complete stop.

C

Carbon Monoxide – Odorless, colorless, potentially lethal gas that is in your exhaust fumes.

Collision – When two or more objects meet forcefully.

Controlled Intersection – Where stop signs or lights control the traffic where streets or roads meet.

Controlled Railroad Crossing – Flashing red lights and gates that control railroad crossings.

Cover the Brake – Holding your foot over the brake to be ready to use it quickly if necessary.

Crossbuck – An X-shaped sign located next to uncontrolled railroad crossings.

D

Deceleration Lane – A lane to use to slow down to take a exit ramp off an expressway or toll way.

Defensive Driving – To drive so you protect yourself and others from dangerous driving situations.

Driving Under the Influence (DUI) – Driving while alcohol or drugs are in your system impairing your driving ability.

E

Entrance Ramp – A slanted road that leads you onto an expressway.

Exit Ramp – A ramp that leads you off an expressway.

F

Field Sobriety Test – A roadside test that allows a police officer determine if you are impaired or intoxicated.

Flashing Signal – Tells a driving when to stop or to proceed with caution.

Force of Impact – The force level at which one object hits another.

Four-Second Following Rule – The safe distance to be kept between yourself and the vehicle you are following.

Fresh Green Light – A traffic light that has just turned green.

Friction – The force that keeps your tire from slipping on the road.

G
Guide Sign – A sign that gives you directions to services and other information.

Gravity – The force that pulls objects back to the ground.

H
Hand-Over-Hand Steering – Using both hands to turn the wheel, with one hand crossing over the other to make turns.

Hazard Lights – When your turn signals all flash at the same time as a warning.

Head Restraints – A devise installed on the top-of your seat behind your head to prevent whiplash.

Highway Hypnosis – A sleepy condition that occurs while long-distance driving when you stare at the white lines on the road for hours on end.

Hydroplaning – When your car skates across the top of water on the road and you feel no traction.

I
Implied Consent Law – As soon as you sign your license, you are agreeing to a sobriety test if asked to perform one by an officer of the law.

J

Jack – A device used to lift your vehicle when you need to change a tire or perform maintenance work.

K

L

Lane Signal – A light that lets you know if an expressway lane can or cannot be used.

M

Median – An area separating traffic going in opposite directions.

Merging Areas – Where vehicles merge to join the flow of traffic.

Minimum Speed Limit – You are not allowed to go slower than a certain posted speed.

N

O

Over-Steer – Turning your steering wheel more than necessary for the situation.

P

Parallel Parking – Parking your vehicle parallel to the curb,

Passive Restraints – An automatic seat belt or an airbag.

Peripheral Vision – Areas of sight to the left and right of one's straight ahead vision line.

Perpendicular Parking – Straight (not angled) parking directly to the left or right.

Point of No Return – The place at which a driver must safely continue on through an intersection.

Protected Left Turn – A green arrow at an intersection allowing a left turn.

Q

R

Reference Point – Lining up your vehicle with certain areas or objects in order to make necessary maneuvers safely.

Regulatory Signs – Signs that tell you what is and is not legally allowed.

Riding the Brake – Continuously pressing your foot on the brake pedal while you are driving in an effort to be cautious.

Right of Way – Giving or having immediately access to the road.

Right Turn on Red – Treat it like a stop. Check for traffic, and then proceed when clear (unless prohibited).

Risk – The chance of danger or harm that could result in a collision.

Roadway Markings – Markings on the road that give your direction or warn you.

Rumble Strips – Corrugated strips of concrete embedded in the road that alert drivers of upcoming toll booths, stop signs, or lights, or that define the edge of the road.

Runaway Ramp – An upward escape ramp off mountainous roads where trucks that need to slow down and cannot are assisted to do so.

S

School Zone – A posted area near schools where drivers must travel at 20 miles per hour or less when children are present.

Space Cushion – The space you leave between your vehicle and others around you.

Stale Green Light – A traffic light that has been green for a long period of time.

T

Tail-Gate – When one car is following another too closely for safety and comfort.

Traction – Vehicle tires gripping the roadway.

Traffic Signal – Any series of lights used to control traffic at intersections.

Tread – The surface of your tire that grips the road.

Tunnel Vision – Just seeing the area straight ahead of you and not to the sides.

Turnabout – A maneuver used to turn your car around to go in the opposite direction.

U

Uncontrolled Intersections – An intersection that has not lights or signs regulating it.

Uncontrolled Railroad Crossings – A railroad crossing that has no gates or lights regulating it.

Unprotected Left Turn – Where a vehicle must wait to turn because oncoming traffic has right of way.

V

W

Warning Signs – Signs that alert you to possible conflicts or hazardous situations.

Wolf Pack – A group of vehicles traveling in a close cluster on an expressway.

<u>X</u>

<u>Y</u>

Yield – Allowing another vehicle to go before you.

<u>Z</u>

Zero-Tolerance Law – No one under 21 is allowed to have alcohol in their system.

IN CASE OF A COLLISION

Please keep this in your glove box to use if you have a collision so that you can record all the details that may be necessary if the case goes to court. (Please keep a pen along with this form – it's really hard to write in blood!) Stay safe, and remember to always drive using the four C's: Courtesy, Caution, Common Sense and Confidence.

Date _____

Time _____

Weather Conditions _____

Road Conditions _____

DESCRIBE THE VEHICLES:

Year/Make/Model			
Tag # & State			
Damages			

DESCRIBE THE OTHER PEOPLE:

	DRIVER	PASSENGER	PASSENGER
Name			
Address			
Telephone			
License # & State			
Insurance Company			
Policy Number			
Medical Condition			
Intoxicated?			
Where Seated?			
Wearing Seatbelts?			
Hair Color / Eye Color			
Height / Weight			
Other			

DESCRIBE ANY WITNESSES:

	1	2	3
Name			
Address			
Telephone(s)			
Tag # & State			
Where Standing?			

Road Sign Quiz

IDENTIFICATION OF SIGNS, SHAPES, AND COLORS

The meaning of any sign is indicated by its shape and color. Place the correct number in the space below the sign/shape/color.

1. Yield Right of Way
2. Winding Road
3. Railroad Warning
4. Side Road
5. Signal Ahead
6. No Right Turn
7. Reduction in Lanes

8. Merge
9. No Passing Zone
10. School Zone & School Crossing
11. Pedestrian Crossing
12. Crossroad
13. No U Turn
14. Do Not Enter
15. Road Construction/Maintenance Crossing

16. Stop
17. Slow Moving Vehicle
18. Keep to Right
19. Hill
20. Bicycle Crossing
21. Slippery When Wet
22. No Left Turn

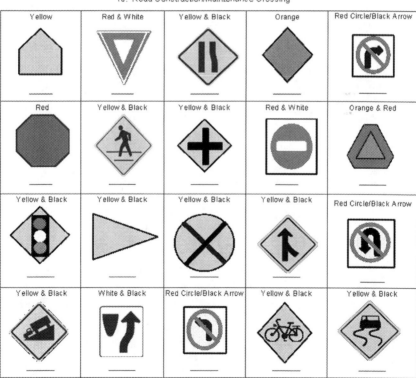